Mortgage Freedom

Retire House Rich and Cash Rich

SANDY AITKEN,
B.Eng., AMP

INSOMNIAC PRESS

Library and Archives Canada Cataloguing in Publication

Aitken, Alexander "Sandy", 1965-
    Mortgage freedom : retire house rich and cash rich / Alexander "Sandy" Aitken.

Includes index.
ISBN 978-1-55483-017-6

1. Mortgage loans--Canada. 2. Finance, Personal--Canada. I. Title.

HG2040.5.C2A57 2011   332.7'220971   C2011-900340-6

AIT

The publisher gratefully acknowledges the support of the Department of Canadian
Heritage through the Book Publishing Industry Development Program.

Printed and bound in Canada

Insomniac Press
520 Princess Avenue,
London, Ontario, Canada, N6B 2B8
www.insomniacpress.com

Canadä

Disclaimer

To my lovely wife, Kim, without whose faith and
encouragement this book would have been written anyway,
and to my two-year-old son, Alex (aka "Wee Man"),
without whose love and attention this book would
have been finished much sooner.

What Canadian homeowners are saying about the Tax Deductible Mortgage Plan (TDMP)....

When I first heard of the TDMP, I thought it was too good to be true. I spent the next two months researching and asking questions. If I received any answers that would cause me concern, I would investigate until I was confident that this indeed was a great plan. Even during the recession when our investments tumbled, history had always shown that with time the economy recovers. The TDMP works on the principle that it needs time, not as much as a conventional mortgage, but time nevertheless. It also saves you a tremendous amount of interest that comes with paying a conventional mortgage on a normal amortization schedule. I read *Rich Dad Poor Dad* and *The Smith Manoeuvre* to help me understand the process. I realized I was an "old school" and conservative thinker when it came to investing and buying a house. I explain the TDMP to people who are interested and I can see that they have reservations much like I did, and I can only say educate yourself on the plan and talk to others who are doing it. It sounds complicated at first, but once you get it and implement it, you will be thrilled you did!

Joanne
Caledon, Ontario

We heard about the Tax Deductible Mortgage Plan via a postcard in the mail. Prior to that, we had not heard of this approach. After attending a TDMP seminar, we found that we couldn't really poke any holes in the concept, so we signed up, although in the back of our minds, we were still wondering if it was too good to be true. After more than three years in the program, we are pleased to say that it has met or exceeded every one of our expectations. Things have basically gone without a hitch. We wholeheartedly recommend the TDMP to everyone with the means to do it.

George and Jeanette G.
Calgary, Alberta

I have many clients from across Canada who participate in the TDMP program. They are able to capitalize on the equity in their home to significantly reduce their tax burden on an ongoing basis. While the TDMP has made the process seamless and pain-free, it is important to ensure each individual program is maintained within Canada Revenue Agency rules. Strict monitoring of the cash flow cycle and proper tax treatment of the income streams and investment loans are essential. This may be manageable by some, but I strongly encourage participation in the TDMP cash flow management program and tax preparation by a qualified professional knowledgeable in this area.

Scott Gray, CMA
Oakville, Ontario

For us, the TDMP has been the best financial investment we have ever made. After we first signed up, I still had reservations and I will admit for the first year I kept expecting "the other shoe to drop." But to my relief it didn't. Everything has and still does work exactly the way the TDMP said it would, with no surprises. I've grown comfortable with this program and I highly recommend this to anyone. We would not feel confident in taking on a program like this and attempting to manage it all by ourselves. It's much too complicated, especially for us. In order for things to flow smoothly, it takes a team to make it work. The TDMP is our team and we appreciate all the behind-the-scenes work that happens on our behalf. I feel strongly supported by the entire team at the TDMP. Kristie is wonderful to work with. Scott makes the whole tax return thing easy and stress-free. Kudos to our financial advisor, Spencer, who has made it possible to look forward to a comfortable retirement in the not-too-distant future.

Anne & Don T.
Calgary, Alberta

Contents

Foreword

Once upon a time, I was the first journalist to review a then-little-known self-published book called *The Smith Manoeuvre*. In it, Fraser Smith described the technique bearing his name about how Canadians can emulate Americans and make their home mortgages tax-deductible.

The movement started in Western Canada and made its way east. Even now, Smith's marketing materials and web site features a column I wrote about it, headlined "Strategy looks like a revolution."

And I guess it was. It captured the attention of Sandy Aitken, the author of the book you now hold in your hand.

Aitken is a hardheaded Scot with a good business head on his shoulders and a sardonic sense of humour. He took the Smith Manoeuvre and automated it in a way that eases the process for the financial advisors and mortgage brokers charged with implementing the strategy on behalf of their retail clients.

Rather than dub it the "Aitken Manoeuvre," Aitken went with the self-explanatory Tax Deductible Mortgage Plan, or the TDMP.

As I wrote about Smith's strategy, I wasn't sure the full enchilada was applicable to all Canadians. I advocated what I called a "Half Smith," which is simply paying down the mortgage. That's what most of the aspiring wealthy boomers I know did in the '80s and '90s, living frugally on two incomes, with the second one devoted to paying off the principal in a few years. When that was accomplished, that was our idea of freedom, reminiscent of the mortgage-burning ceremonies our Depression-era parents performed.

So I was more skeptical about the second half of the Smith Manoeuvre, which was the wealth-creating part that depends on borrowing money to invest. My personal stance, articulated in my own book, *Findependence Day*, was to simply pay off your mortgage as quickly as possible, along with all other consumer debts, starting with student loans and credit cards.

Then, I reasoned, all that cash flow formerly devoted to servicing debt could be redirected into investments: with a healthy allocation to stocks and growth-oriented investments.

Smith was happy with my "half endorsement," but Aitken endeavoured to show me the error of my conservative ways. He gave me a copy of a book called *Lifecycle Investing*, a *New York Times* bestselling book (in 2010) by Ian Ayres and Barry Nalebuff.

The book describes a "free lunch" phenomenon called time diversification and it amounts to a recommendation that young people embrace leverage in order to maximize the time value of money. The longer the time horizon, the authors argue, the less the risk from stocks, leveraged or not.

This is clearly relevant to the full iteration of the TDMP. If you believe this, then you agree life is too short to defer investing in the stock market until you pay off all your debts. The sooner you invest, the faster the magic of compounding can work to your advantage and build wealth.

By simultaneously paying down a mortgage and then applying the interest savings to the market, you create a virtuous cycle of decreasing debt and rising wealth. As anyone will tell you, that's the recipe for increasing your net worth.

The bonus is that the taxman provides a little extra rocket fuel on that moon shot to wealth: by converting non-tax-deductible mortgage debt to tax-deductible investment loans, you should be able to speed the arrival of your Findependence Day!

When I agreed to write this foreword, the working title was *Mortgage Freedom*. I suggested a more apt title for this book would be *House Rich, Cash Rich*, which implies you can have your home and money too if you play your cards correctly.

Aitken and Smith think that by being too conservative, you'll end up house rich but cash poor. They paint the dire picture of the destitute senior whose only major asset is their home, which they may eventually be forced to tap via a reverse mortgage.

The point, I suppose, is that as the FRAM Filter ads say, you can pay now or pay later. If indeed your home is one of your biggest assets, then the sooner you tap the equity to create wealth, the better.

In retrospect, had the TDMP been available when I was paying down my mortgage in the '80s, my own mortgage freedom might have arrived earlier.

For homeowners today, there can be no guarantees, but *Mortgage Freedom* does lay out a roadmap to put the odds in your favor.

Jonathan Chevreau is the National Post*'s personal finance columnist. He also writes the daily Wealthy Boomer blog, and is the author of* Findependence Day: One Couple's Turbulent Journey to Financial Independence.

Preface

This is a book about achieving financial success. I wrote it because too many Canadian families are struggling to save enough money for retirement. In my analysis, this often happens because it takes too long to pay off a mortgage. This book describes a financial strategy that is helpful to those who take their personal finances seriously. It is an essential read for those who are actively planning to be both wealthier *and* mortgage-free at retirement.

Achieving mortgage freedom is a lifelong journey. Whether you are in your twenties and thinking about purchasing your first home, or whether you are in your forties or fifties and thinking about how to fund your lifestyle in retirement, there is something in this book for you. You could read this book cover to cover, but the most efficient way to review it is to read the Introduction and then jump to the stage that best describes your own personal situation.

As a computer engineer, I've been building software in

the mortgage and real estate industries for over twenty years. As the owner of a mortgage brokerage and TDMP.com, I have seen firsthand how misguided conventional wisdom or the lack of financial planning costs homeowners thousands of dollars in unnecessary mortgage interest and income taxes every year. This money rightfully belongs in the hands of the individuals who earned it. This book shows Canadian taxpayers how to stop the bleeding and redirect their hard-earned cash into building their nest eggs.

I had a lot of help writing this book. I would like to thank my publisher, Insomniac Press, and Mike O'Connor in particular, for the initial inspiration and for setting me to my purpose. I would also like to thank the managing editor, Dan Varrette, for relentlessly pressing me forward and for translating the bits and bytes of engineer-speak into something that more closely resembles English.

I would like to thank my parents for their support and their input, especially my father, Alexander Aitken, whose expertise as a lawyer and author was invaluable. I also had some help from the team at TDMP.com head office. Thanks so much for reading and advising on the various versions of the manuscript as it evolved. A special thanks to Jason, Brad, Alan, Kristie and, of course, to my brother and business partner, George Aitken, for editing and encouraging this project along and for allowing me the time required to complete this book.

I also extend my appreciation to Rodney Clark of claremontconsulting.ca for his keen insight into mortgages held inside RRSPs and to Jonathan Chevreau, the country's leading personal finance columnist, for contributing the Foreword and for dreaming up the subtitle to this book. I thank my learned friend Calum Ross, a Harvard-educated expert in real estate and Canada's number one mortgage broker, for his incisive intellect, expertise, and constructive feedback and for contributing the Afterword.

Last and most important, thanks so much to my wonderful wife, Kim, and my boy, Alex "Wee Man" Aitken, who just turned two years old. Notwithstanding my tongue-in-cheek dedication of this book, writing has made an absentee father and husband out of me for the better part of a year, even when I was home. I'm so very grateful to have such a patient, understanding, happy wife and such a genius for a son. Thanks for your support, Kimmy, you really are the greatest!

Introduction

Mortgage freedom might sound like a self-explanatory financial goal. We are all mortgage-free until the day we purchase our first home. In that instant, you realize that the dream of homeownership is only possible with the assistance of your friendly mortgage bank. Everyone knows that from the day you purchased your first home, you will embark on a multi-decade journey to become mortgage-free once again.

If you consider a definition of *financial freedom* to mean having enough money to do what you like, then mortgage freedom becomes more than just paying off your mortgage. Mortgage freedom is about building enough wealth (outside of your home) to retire comfortably on your own schedule. When you're retired, you need the financial wherewithal to be master of your own time because you're effectively unemployed. To ensure a comfortable retirement, you need to do more than just pay off your mortgage; you must also have a reliable source of steady income that allows you to live the lifestyle you have become used to.

When is it wise to borrow money? If you're like most Canadians, you will agree that purchasing your first home is one of the best times to get a loan. All young people need a mortgage when they buy their first home, and it seems to work out quite well for most families in the long run. Why, then, are we so decidedly less enthusiastic about borrowing to invest for retirement? Canadians view the very notion of borrowing to invest with a healthy dose of skepticism, and the practice seems to have fallen outside the realm of generally acceptable behaviour. Somehow, we have been conditioned to believe that borrowing to invest must be a risky or speculative endeavour. How unfortunate! The idea that borrowing to invest is always riskier than not borrowing is a clear misconception and it probably explains why so many Canadian homeowners are failing to save enough money to retire. Sadly, too many ordinary Canadians will work hard for forty years or more only to end up being house rich and cash poor and wondering why. Maybe it's time to challenge the traditional way of thinking about mortgages and financing.

The experts universally agree that when it comes to investing, the best thing you can do is diversify. Mutual funds are credited with solving the problem of diversification across all asset classes and geography, but what about diversification over time? Temporal diversification in retirement portfolios continues to elude too many of us and is the root cause of shortfall in many retirement funds.

The average working life is about forty years. Conventional wisdom dictates that you should pay off your mortgage before you start to save for retirement. This serial approach to investing means that most of us won't begin saving for retirement until we are in our fifties. When you consider that the equity markets can actually lose money over any ten-year period, as they have several times in history, including the last decade, you may come to realize that waiting until your mortgage is fully paid off before you start saving for retirement presents a problem. You may not have enough time to accumulate the wealth you need to retire comfortably on your own schedule.

Ian Ayres and Barry Nalebuff are professors at the Yale School of Management and are the *New York Times* best-selling authors who wrote the book *Lifecycle Investing*. In their book, they prove that you can reduce risk and build a larger retirement portfolio by starting earlier with borrowed money. In Canada, it's perfectly acceptable and commonplace to leverage your home, sometimes as high as 19:1, using a high-ratio mortgage with the minimum 5% down payment. Canadians unanimously believe, with great confidence, that if you become a homeowner early and continue to own for thirty years or more, you will pay off your mortgage and your home will have drastically increased in value due to inflation. The dream of lifelong homeownership is alive and well in Canada, and our universal belief in the inevitability of its unparalleled success is hardwired into our financial psyche from birth.

So why don't we have the same confidence in our retirement plans? The fact is that the equity markets have drastically outperformed the housing market throughout our lifetimes, but we don't feel that this is the case. All appearances and practical experience tell us that real estate must somehow be a better investment than the stock market because, generally speaking, we seem to do better in real estate. If you believe this, you're delusional. It's a myth. Although the great majority of Canadian baby boomers have enjoyed several decades of heavily leveraged exposure to the real estate market through their homes, they have failed miserably to apply the same principles to leveraging their retirement funds. If you're successful in homeownership but otherwise feeling short of cash in your long-term financial plan, you now know the reason. But it's never too late! A proven mortgage strategy for your home can only work better for your retirement fund.

Mortgage Freedom is a financial strategy that shows you how to transfer the leverage from your home to your retirement fund, to build greater wealth with less risk, *and* be debt-free sooner.

Ayres and Nalebuff based *Lifecycle Investing* on an empirical study where they proved conclusively that if you borrow money to start investing in equities when you're young, your retirement fund will be 35% larger with 20% less risk. Furthermore, you can expect to be 63% wealthier at retirement if you conservatively leverage (e.g. 2:1) at a young age taking the exact same portfolio risk as someone who waits until they can afford to actually save for retirement. This study was conducted and validated across 138 years of market data from 1871 to 2009 and was proven to hold true over any generational period.

Canadians are already borrowing vast sums of money to purchase their homes. *Mortgage Freedom* does not necessarily advocate that young people take on more leverage than they are already committed to through homeownership. *Mortgage Freedom* is simply a practical guide for Canadians on how to transfer debt from your home to your retirement fund in a manner that will ensure that you achieve your long-term financial goals and generate significant tax benefits along the way.

Mortgage Freedom is one solution for Canadian homeowners who desire to be both free of their mortgage and wealthier at retirement without using their own cash. Read this book and you will learn how to finance your retirement using only the equity in your home and none of your own hard-earned income.

What's Your Number?

How much money will you need to enjoy a comfortable retirement? One million dollars? Two million? Three? The answer will vary widely among individuals, but a good barometer is twenty times the amount of income that you plan to spend each year after you retire. For example, if you think you can live on $100,000 per year, you will need to have saved $2 million, not including your home, to retire with no financial concerns. Any shortfall will result in the steady erosion of your precious cash reserves. As you watch your nest egg dwindle away, year over year, your retirement becomes a race—a race that you can only win by kicking the bucket before you run out of money. Now does that sound like a comfortable retirement to you?

If the thought of saving millions of dollars from your salary completely blows your mind, don't sweat it; there is a solution. The younger you are, the more natural it is that "your number" for retirement will seem like a fantastic sum of money, especially when you think about actually saving it up from your own scarce financial resources. After all, if you are practical in the assessment of your number, it likely equates to something like ten or twenty years of your current gross annual income.

If you follow the financial journey to mortgage freedom described in the four distinct stages of this book, your funds for retirement may be substantially generated for you without using any of your own savings. A key objective of the *Mortgage Freedom* strategy is to ensure that your tax savings and investment gains are carefully cultivated, reinvested, and grown over time so that you can retire in excellent financial shape. After all, what choice do you really have? You cannot possibly save ten years' salary in your lifetime. In fact, you would be a rare breed if you could even save one year's salary over the next five years. The reason why it's so hard to save your salary is because you need it—or at least most of it—just to meet your monthly obligations.

As a taxpayer and homeowner, it's your depressing reality that the government and the bank will likely take most of your gross monthly income. The government will come for the lion's share, at least 50% or more of your gross pay in one form of taxes or another. Canadian income taxes can exceed 46% at the margin in some provinces, but even if your income tax is 35% or less, as a homeowner, you will also have to pay property taxes, which will increase your overall personal tax bill significantly. When you add GST/HST, gas tax, liquor tax, tire tax, and all the other hidden taxes we pay, it's safe to say that a minimum of 50% of your gross income will go to one level of government or another in the form of taxes. The second biggest slice out of your hard-earned salary will go to your banker. When you first get a mortgage, your mortgage payment will account for 35% or 40% of your total income, which leaves only 10% or 15% of your salary available to save—assuming that you don't need to eat!

David Chilton's top tip in his book *The Wealthy Barber* is to "pay yourself first." However, the practical reality for most homeowners in this country is that you pay the government first (50% in taxes), your banker next (35% for your mortgage payment), then you feed your family and pay the bills (10% to 15%), and, finally, if there's anything left, you pay yourself—last.

Whether your number for retirement is one million dollars or five, the question remains the same. How are you going to create the kind of wealth you will need in the future when you can't save it from your income? You definitely need some help.

The equity you build in your home is likely going to be the single largest asset that you will ever accumulate. After all, we all need to live somewhere, and the capital gain in your principal residence will grow tax-free forever without exception. There is no better deal than that. However, when you decide to become an investor, as well as a homeowner, your home equity becomes a strategic asset that will provide you the opportunity to generate far greater wealth for you and your family if properly managed.

Are You a Canadian NINJA?

Have you heard of a NINJA mortgage? NINJA stands for No Income, No Job, (No) Assets. NINJA mortgages achieved infamy in the U.S. in 2008 as they epitomized what has become widely known as the U.S. subprime mortgage crisis. Fortunately, in Canada, there is no such thing as a NINJA mortgage. NINJA has a much different connotation and it relates more closely to retirement. Traditionally, Canadians have been taught that they should diligently pay off their mortgages before they retire, and many Canadians plan to pay off their mortgages and retire simultaneously, celebrating both events by "burning the mortgage" on the day they stop working. We call this the Canadian NINJA Plan.

You're a Canadian NINJA if your plan is to pay off your mortgage and retire on the same day with **No Income** (because you just retired), **No Job** (because you just retired), and no **Assets** (outside of your home which is paid for), and as long as you have no expenses for the rest of your life, the Canadian NINJA Plan might just work out quite well for your retirement. However, you can see the problem. The Canadian NINJA has single-handedly created a market for reverse mortgages in Canada because if you plan to retire with no assets, or any other source of income, you will immediately find yourself needing to tap the equity in your home just to meet your monthly expenses and pay your property taxes. The bad news for the NINJA is that immediately upon retirement, you will no longer qualify for a regular "prime" mortgage or line of credit. This means the more expensive reverse mortgage may be your only financial option short of actually selling your home.

Fortunately, the majority of Canadian homeowners now realize that a plan to pay off your mortgage on the day you retire is a plan to fail! The Canadian NINJA Plan is an unmitigated personal financial disaster. To avoid a NINJA retirement, you need a parallel investment plan that allows you to begin saving for your long-term financial needs long before you have actually paid off your mortgage.

Mortgage Trends

Canadians have an international reputation for being such nice people. It's almost annoying. At home, we're not so different, and the lenders know that the typical Canadian homebuyer is prone to politely accept the standard terms of whatever home loan is first offered to them. It's simply not in our nature to haggle—especially about something we don't fully understand. We might be inclined to have some cordial banter with our banker with respect to the interest rate that they are offering, but otherwise, we will readily accept the fact that mortgage terms must somehow be standardized and are not to be negotiated with any real enthusiasm by a borrower.

In light of this, your schedule to being mortgage-free will be quite predictable. In the absence of any accelerated payments, you can anticipate burning your mortgage at the end of your amortization period.

Canadian mortgage terms range from six months to ten years. A five-year term is the most common, and each time the mortgage term expires, the homeowner will typically renew it into another five-year term at the then prevailing five-year fixed rate. This cycle will repeat itself until the amortization period concludes and the mortgage is paid off. Along the way, the average family will purchase a new home two or three times in their lifetime. Each time they purchase a new home, the mortgage debt and the correspon-ding payments are adjusted in direct correlation to the new mortgage balance.

The simple act of renewing a mortgage every five years, or every time you purchase a new home, is not in itself a strategic plan. This is a plan that best serves the lender and provides no real benefit to the homeowner. The only sure way to accelerate your path to being debt-free in this scenario is to make extra mortgage payments from your own after-tax income. Many Canadians already accelerate their mortgage payments by moving to a bi-weekly accel-erated payment schedule. It's widely known that this will knock years off a mortgage and it's a good strategy for those who can afford it, but it still doesn't build your retirement nest egg.

An alarming new mortgage trend developed in 2006 when the Canadian federal government shocked everyone when they relaxed the rules by extending the longest amortization period (the maximum duration over which you can pay off your mortgage) from twenty-five to forty years. The government subsequently shortened it to thirty-five years in 2008, and for high-ratio borrowers, it was again reduced to thirty years in January 2011. However, a consumer study[1] showed that 42% of the mortgages originated in 2010 are amortizing over the full thirty-five-year period. That brings the total number of Canadian homeowners with mortgages that amortize longer than twenty-five years up to a whopping 1.24 million (or 22% of all mortgaged homes) from zero in a short four-year period. Although the federal government has tightened the rules three times since 2008, it's reasonable to expect that the trend towards using the maximum available amortization will continue, in which case, the vast majority of residential mortgages in Canada will likely be amortizing over a thirty or thirty-five-year period by the time you read this book. In the absence of an accelerated payment schedule, or an effective mortgage strategy to pay it off sooner, many of these homeowners will take the full thirty-five years to become debt-free.

There are some obvious benefits to a mortgage with a longer amortization period. A mortgage that a borrower pays out over thirty-five years instead of the traditional twenty-five years provides flexibility to the borrower, a slower payout to the lender, and clearly promotes Canadian homeownership in general. By lowering the payments and reducing the monthly financial burden, your cash flow will definitely improve in the short term. The insurance premium charged to borrowers for the benefit of having this extra ten years to pay off the mortgage is relatively inexpensive, which indicates that the actuarial experts must believe that longer amortizations will not significantly increase the risk that homeowners will default on their mortgages. Whatever the reason, there can be no arguing the popularity of longer amortizing mortgages when you consider the staggering rate of their adoption by Canadian mortgage lenders, insurers, and homebuyers alike.

The benefits of a longer amortization to all stakeholders are clear enough, but the impact of these longer-term mortgages on individual retirement plans is not so obvious. There are 4.4 million Canadians with shorter amortizing mortgages (less than twenty-five years), and according to the survey, they plan to be debt-free by age forty-seven on average. The other 1.24 million Canadians (with amortizations longer than twenty-five years) don't plan to be debt-free until age fifty-three on average. The problem is that both those groups of borrowers are planning to retire at the same age: sixty-one years old! Planning to save enough money for retirement in this short eight-year period is a plan to fail if ever there was one.

If you're one of these million-plus homeowners who plan to have your mortgage paid off at age fifty-three and retire at age sixty-one, perhaps you haven't thought things through properly. Part of the problem is that Canadians are generally living much longer than previous generations. Currently, the life expectancy for a Canadian couple that reach the age of sixty-two is twenty more years for a man and twenty-seven for a woman. As you can see, women are outliving men in this country, but the more salient point is that prudent financial planning for retirement equates to finding the financial means required to fund a lifestyle for both spouses through thirty years or more of life after work.

A Strategic Approach

Historically, the terms of a Canadian mortgage loan have confined homeowners to a relentless systematic schedule of pre-authorized principal and interest payments until the mortgage is finally paid off. The process of paying off a mortgage can take two or three decades or more, especially when you consider that most homeowners will buy bigger homes several times during their lives, adding more debt to the mortgage each time. During this extended period of mortgaged homeownership, if you had wished to become an investor, either in your own business or in the businesses of others, you would naturally have done so using your own savings or other personal assets. In past years, there has been no practical opportunity to leverage your home equity for investment purposes while you were still paying off your mortgage. Fortunately for today's Canadian homeowner, the mortgage landscape has improved drastically and presents many helpful financial options that you can use to ensure that you retire comfortably.

The two major changes that give homeowners and investors the ability to manage their personal finances more effectively in the twenty-first century are based in technological advances in the mortgage industry combined with improvements in Canadian tax laws that benefit the individual.

First, technology and innovation have enabled mortgage lenders, in a highly competitive environment, to create more flexible home loan products with practical features that borrowers can apply to managing debt with tax efficiency and to build wealth. Specifically, the invention of the multi-component re-advanceable home equity line of credit (HELOC) allows borrowers to start investing for their retirement earlier by repurposing their mortgage debt. This subject is covered in the section entitled Stage II: Invest

Early and Often.

Second, the Canadian courts have made a series of key decisions that increasingly favour the individual taxpayer's fundamental right to actively manage their financial affairs in a manner that reduces their income-tax burden. They also guarantee tax deductions against income tax as your reward for becoming an investor and supporting the Canadian economy. You can safely apply the cash you receive back from the taxman to paying down your mortgage sooner, and when you reinvest, it will build greater wealth for your retirement. This subject is also covered in Stage II.

The Canadian Story

Many factors have come together over the last decade to effectively enable Canadians to embark on a more lucrative journey to mortgage freedom. Powerful financial strategies that allow homeowners to build wealth by tax-efficiently leveraging debt were simply not available a mere decade ago and were unimaginable in the previous century. We appreciate that the credit for this evolution must be shared among technology-enabled innovation, favourable tax decisions, economists, financial gurus, and the entrepreneurs who have successfully paved the road for a brighter future in homeownership. Canadian homeowners are the real beneficiaries of the efforts of a few pioneers and innovators and, as a result, we are all privileged to pursue a far more lucrative path to a wealthier retirement in the twenty-first century. The Canadian story told here is a brief history of the contributions of key individuals and corporations that have paved the way to more effective retirement planning and wealth building in this country.

The Smith Manoeuvre—A Canadian Inspiration

At the turn of the century, a west coast financial advisor named Fraser Smith earned much of the early credit for being the first to publicly ask the provocative question, "Is your mortgage tax-deductible?" At the time of its first publication, Smith's book *The Smith Manoeuvre* instantly became the nation's leading advocate of mortgage debt conversion for tax deductibility in Canada.

In his book, Smith explains the core concept of converting mortgage debt into an investment loan and the resulting benefits to the taxpayer. He also goes on to discuss some technical aspects on the subject of capitalizing interest and how to structure your debt for tax efficiency, as well as how to talk to your banker about doing this for you. As far back as thirty years ago, without the benefit of modern technology and innovative mortgage products, Smith and other financial advisors across the country had to make special arrangements with bankers on behalf of their customers in order to convert a regular Canadian mortgage into a tax-deductible investment line of credit. In those days, this was a tremendously complex and time-consuming undertaking.

These savvy financial advisors, in partnership with a cooperative lender, would hobble together a line of credit with a mortgage in such a manner that would allow the execution of the Smith Manoeuvre, effectively transforming a regular (non-tax-deductible) mortgage into a tax-deductible loan over a period of years or decades. In concept, the Smith Manoeuvre is a sound debt-conversion strategy that has been proven to make Canadian homeowners wealthier. In practice, it was too difficult for most ordinary Canadian homeowners to either understand or administer.

The Smith Manoeuvre didn't really achieve the level of popularity it could have, mostly because homeowners trying to execute it were faced with a number of excursions to their bank branch each and every month to write cheques, transfer funds, and keep the strategy on track. Fortunately, those days are well behind us.

The good news for today's Canadian borrowers is that they no longer have to sweat many of these administrative details when structuring their debt for tax efficiency. Innovation in the mortgage industry has seen the introduction of a whole new breed of mortgages and lines of credit, some of which can be employed to execute rudimentary debt-management strategies right out of the box. Gone is the requirement to make special requests and proprietary arrangements with your local bank branch manager. Today, many mortgage professionals are able to arrange the kind of mortgage/line of credit that you would need to self-administer a very basic Smith Manoeuvre style of debt-conversion strategy. Information on these mortgage experts and lenders can be found at www.mortgagefreedom.ca.

Technology and innovation are not the only things that have improved by leaps and bounds to the benefit of Canadian consumers. Our understanding of the Income Tax Act, through key court decisions and subsequent technical bulletins from the Canadian Revenue Agency (CRA), have permanently changed how we understand consumer debt— and for the better.

Ten years ago, tax-deductible mortgages had not really been formally tested or determined by the courts, and the CRA often looked down upon and aggressively reassessed them. Times have changed. A series of court decisions, including several pivotal determinations by the Supreme Court of Canada, have consistently supported, defined, and upheld the rights of Canadian taxpayers and given the federal government's tax collector, the CRA, clear instructions in this regard.

This is all good news for homeowners. When *The Smith Manoeuvre* was first published, it was a very popular bestseller. But the mortgage products of the day made execution of the manoeuvre overly complicated and administratively onerous, which limited the popularity of this powerful mortgage strategy.

Now that the question about tax deductibility of interest on loans has been clarified and approved by the Canadian courts and the CRA, the adoption of tax-efficient debt strategies in Canada is back on the rise. Canadian taxpayers' fundamental right to arrange their financial affairs to reduce the tax they are required to pay is now enshrined in Canadian tax law and effective tax planning should form the basis of every mortgaged homeowner's long-term financial plan.

The landscape has finally improved in favour of the little guy. The individual borrower and taxpayer can now confidently take advantage of all Canadian tax deductions (including appropriate mortgage interest deductibility) and retain more of their hard-earned income to pay down the mortgage and build personal wealth.

Economists, Authors, and Financial Gurus

Jonathan Chevreau is one of Canada's leading personal finance columnists, writing regularly for the *Financial Post* and posting on his blog, The Wealthy Boomer. Chevreau is a great advocate of the ordinary Canadian's noble endeavour to build enough wealth to retire comfortably. In his 2008 book *Findependence Day*, Chevreau defines the date you achieve "financial independence" in a fictional account of an ordinary Canadian family's lifelong pursuit of this coveted financial goal. Just in case you missed it, the title word *findependence* is a clever contraction of the goal: financial independence.

In a sense, one might consider *Mortgage Freedom* as one practical path on a journey to your Findependence Day. As a book with a compelling narrative, you may find *Findependence Day* a more entertaining read than a no-nonsense non-fiction narrative about mortgages and taxes. *Findependence Day* is recommended reading for new homeowners and younger readers interested in all aspects of their personal finances.

In *Findependence Day*, Chevreau makes reference to Dr. Moshe Milevsky's book *Are You a Stock or a Bond?* where Milevsky argues that you should look at your wealth as a combination of your current net worth and your future earnings. As a finance professor at York University in Toronto for almost twenty years, Milevsky explains that the real wealth of many young people, who have little or no savings, is actually in the millions of dollars that they will earn in their lifetimes. Milevsky uses the term *human capital* to describe the present value of your future earnings and credits Professor Gary Becker, the 1992 Nobel Laureate in Economics, with the original concept.

The Yale professors Ian Ayers and Barry Nalebuff, who authored *Lifecycle Investing*, take a slightly different approach and argue that your current wealth is equal to your current savings plus the present value of your future savings (as opposed to future earnings). They dedicate their work to their teacher, America's first Nobel Prize winner Paul Samuelson, who convincingly argued that you should allocate your investments based on your lifetime wealth, not just your current savings. This simple yet brilliant insight inspired them to undertake a painstaking analysis of 138 years of historical market data from which they concluded that if young people in their thirties and forties use leverage to invest in their retirement, they will be much wealthier with less risk.

The naysayers on the subject of borrowing to invest have finally been stumped! In a land of free speech, everyone may be entitled to express their own opinions, but no one is entitled to create their own facts. Borrowing money to invest in your retirement may be contrary to the way you have been conditioned to think, but the fact is that it has now been proven a safer and better approach to funding your nest egg.

Hats off to all those who have dared to challenge the establishment and speak out in support of the ordinary person's long term objective of retiring in comfort!

The Tax Deductible Mortgage Plan (TDMP)

The Tax Deductible Mortgage Plan (TDMP) was introduced to the Canadian market by yours truly, the author, Sandy Aitken, and his partners in 2006. Inspired in part by the proven tax benefits of the Smith Manoeuvre, the TDMP was more heavily influenced by the groundbreaking work of the economists and other financial gurus who originally made, and ultimately proved, their case for building a retirement fund using responsible leverage.

The TDMP is a practical Canadian solution to achieving this worthy goal. The underlying premise of the TDMP is that the most convenient and cost effective source of financial leverage is money that you have already borrowed! As a Canadian homeowner, your unique advantage is that if you mortgage your retirement nest egg using the same debt previously used to mortgage your home, you get the added bonus of making your mortgage tax-deductible, which compounds the financial benefits every step of the way.

The TDMP is a completely automated solution for the ordinary Canadian homeowner who wishes to be wealthier at retirement but doesn't want to do the legwork themselves. The TDMP applies the CRA-defined and -approved methods for interest deductibility and is up to five times more powerful due to the technology used and the wholesale agreements with lenders that automate specific services that are often not available to individual borrowers. Homeowners who want the financial benefits of financing their retirement and making their mortgage tax-deductible now have the easy option of engaging the TDMP and letting the professionals handle the details.

To maximize the efficiency of building wealth for retirement, the TDMP employs an accelerator that multiplies the effective rate of debt conversion (from non-deductible debt to deductible debt) by four or five times with a corresponding increase in the wealth of the homeowner. While the mechanics of how to set up and execute the TDMP are described in Stage III of this book, the plan is available to qualified homeowners as a fully managed service at www.tdmp.com. That said, and in the interest of appropriate disclosure, it should be noted that the author of this book is a co-founder, a shareholder, and, at the time of publication, the CEO and President of TDMP.com. Any attempt to write an unbiased review of the TDMP or the services provided by the national network of TDMP Certified Mortgage Planners (listed at www.tdmp.com) would be utterly futile.

The TDMP is the crown jewel in your journey to mortgage freedom, as it will make the largest financial contribution to your retirement nest egg without using your own cash flow. In a typical case where a simple cash-damming strategy would generate $200,000 in net wealth over twenty-five years, you could plan on the TDMP contributing another $1 million or more towards your retirement fund over the same period.

As an investor, the TDMP is where you will get the biggest bang for your buck in your journey to mortgage freedom, as you will effectively be putting your money to work twice. The TDMP is a closed loop, an automated monthly cycle that generates its own cash and automates the reinvestment of all your financial and tax benefits. It's designed to ensure that you can reach your long-term financial goals without investing more of your own cash or doing any of the onerous monthly cash-flow administration that must be attended to on a weekly and monthly basis. The TDMP is currently Canada's only nationwide, managed, debt-conversion service available to qualified Canadian homeowners who want the benefits of converting their mortgage into a tax-deductible investment loan without the hassle. TDMP.com has won numerous mortgage industry awards for their groundbreaking technology and debt-management methods and have appeared multiple times on *Profit Magazine*'s coveted PROFIT 100 list of the fastest growing Canadian companies.

Eligibility for the TDMP requires that you have built up some equity in your home, which needs to be available to invest. Many TDMP homeowners have owned their property for at least a decade, and the equity builds as a combination of the value of their home increasing over time and the mortgage being paid down. If you have been in the workforce for ten or twenty years and owned a home for much of that period, you will probably also find that both your home and your salary have increased in value during this time. If you're in a higher tax bracket and have enough equity in your home, the TDMP will be the most important strategy on your journey to mortgage freedom, as it will contribute the most money to your retirement fund. Find out if you're eligible for the TDMP by taking the TDMP Test at www.tdmp.com.

Mortgage Freedom

The first decade of the twenty-first century was less than stellar with the market crashes of 2002 and 2008. The good news for Canadians is that the outlook for our economy and the growth prospects for our housing market in particular look promising. This might seem like a bold statement in the context of what is happening south of the border. Perhaps, as Canadians, we have been blessed with good fortune, or perhaps our prospects are better for some reason. Let's review.

The American Housing Market

At the start of 2011, the state of the American housing market can fairly be described as an unmitigated disaster. In an interview with Peter Mansbridge on CBC national television, Ed Clark, a senior Canadian bank executive, recently characterized the U.S. housing problem as "incurable." Some people, including the Yale professor Robert Shiller, who created the Standard & Poor's Case-Shiller Home Price Indices and correctly predicted the U.S. housing market meltdown, have speculated that Canada could face a similar situation in the years to come. Rubbish! You may have heard the saying that when the U.S. sneezes, Canada catches a cold. Well, not this time!

While our neighbours to the south struggle with a collapsed housing market and a failed banking system, the state of the housing and mortgage market in Canada has remained strong throughout the recession and continues to grow at a healthy predictable rate in line with house prices and GDP growth. In August 2010, the total residential mortgage debt in Canada broke through the $1 trillion barrier for the first time ever. Growing at a healthy average annual pace of approximately 8%, Canadians have more than doubled their aggregate mortgage debt from $440 billion in less than a decade. Contrary to some fear-mongering media reports, $1 trillion in mortgage debt is actually more manageable than you might think. Unlike our American neighbours, the vast majority of Canadian home-owners can easily afford their mortgage payments, even in the event of a substantial increase in interest rates, which seems very likely in the years to come.

There are other clear distinctions between the Canadian and U.S. residential housing markets. In Canada, you don't get to walk away from your mortgage by handing your house keys back to the bank. In the U.S., not only is this common-place, they even have a name for it: strategic default. The rationale for a strategic default is that when your mortgage balance exceeds the value of your home, you should walk away from both. Even Americans who can afford their mort-gage payments will consider strategically defaulting on their loan if the property value falls below the balance owing and they have no personal liability for the debt. On the other hand, Canadian mortgage loans are full recourse, which means that the borrower is on the hook for the full amount of the debt even if the proceeds from liquidating the property do not cover the outstanding loan balance.

Canada has never promoted the kind of irresponsible lending that was so prolific in the U.S. As mentioned above, the Canadian NINJA in retirement does not allow you to qualify for a mortgage. This is in stark contrast to American

NINJA mortgages, which were loans routinely provided to those with no income, job, or assets. In addition to NINJA mortgages, American innovation created what were called "exotic" mortgages that were designed to lower payments by actually capitalizing the interest and adding it back to the mortgage balance each month over the first couple of years. This uniquely American concept was based on the simple premise that home values would always go up—a premise that, in hindsight, has proven false.

The thinking was that if home values are always on the increase, consistently growing faster than your mortgage balance, then what's the harm? Surely there is no need to actually pay all the interest due each month on the loan. Besides, a lower threshold of entry will allow more Americans to realize the dream of homeownership and that has to be a good thing. When house prices started to fall in 2008, however, the exotic mortgage loans provided to NINJA borrowers led millions of U.S. homeowners who owned properties they couldn't afford to rent, let alone own, into default and foreclosure. This sad story is well documented. As U.S. house prices declined, *NINJA* became a bad word and these "exotic" mortgages rapidly became "toxic" assets in the hands of investors when the payments reset to proper levels of principal and interest after an introductory period. Millions of American homeowners never had a chance. They had taken out loans from lenders on terms they didn't understand—and if they did, it was a risk they would not escape. When the dust settled, these unfortunate borrowers found themselves responsible for mortgage payments they couldn't possibly afford and the natural consequence was that they faced losing their homes.

In 2008, the American dream became a nightmare as the first wave of mortgage defaults and foreclosures swept the country, stopping abruptly at the Canadian border. To understand why Canadian homeowners weren't infected by this distinctly American problem, it's important to realize that the banking systems in our two countries are much different and the reckless irresponsible lending and other economic triggers that set off the U.S. mortgage and housing collapse simply do not exist in Canada.

A Canadian Outlook

In Canada, there has never been any such thing as a U.S.-style exotic mortgage that negatively amortizes by lowering your payments to a mere fraction of the actual interest payable. Most Canadians would find the very concept of having a mortgage balance that grows every month quite appalling. Canadian homeowners have to prove that they can afford their regular principal and interest payments, and strategically defaulting on any debt is not a socially acceptable option in this country, not to mention the fact that lenders would seek a judgement to recover any portion of unpaid mortgage debt in most Canadian provinces. As default rates in the U.S. approached double digits, the Canadian default rates remained at historically normal levels: less than half of one percent.

Canadians homeowners can sleep well at night. While house prices in some Canadian regions may slump from time to time, there is no reason to get excited. As a nation, we continue to have more than adequate equity in our homes, even though our aggregate mortgage debt increases every single year. When our total mortgage debt blew through the $1 trillion mark in August 2010, the value of all the residential property in this country was approaching $4 trillion, which equates to a very robust 72% overall ratio of home equity to debt among all homeowners. The 80/20 rule is alive and well in the Canadian housing market where 81% of borrowers have no less than 20% equity in their home. The fact is that the majority of Canadians can easily afford their mortgage payments with plenty of room to spare, even when interest rates inevitably rise. Unlike Americans, we know that we can afford our mortgages, but the real question is: can we afford to retire on time?

Americans do have a few advantages. One major advantage that U.S. homeowners have over Canadians is that their mortgages are tax-deductible—at least for the time being. For several generations, Americans have universally believed that their entitlement to their mortgage interest deduction was a God-given right and it has formed the cornerstone of every middle-class American homeowner's financial plan for the better part of a century. More recently, the sheer size of the U.S. national debt has policymakers on the warpath to cut the U.S. deficit, and it has become increasingly clear that the sacred status of tax-deductible mortgages in America is in jeopardy. After all, if the original intent of this interest deduction was to drive up home ownership levels, it has failed miserably. The fact is that U.S. homeownership levels lag behind Canadian homeownership levels, and we don't even have a mortgage interest deduction policy. The mortgage interest deduction in the U.S.

burdens the American tax base in excess of $130 billion annually, and one way or another, it's widely anticipated that a good chunk of this tax deduction will be recovered by the U.S. government in future years in order to assist with their overwhelming financial issues.

In light of the pressure that tax-deductible mortgages are coming under in the U.S., the prospect of a Canadian mortgage ever becoming tax-deductible by government decree is so remote as to be negligible. Past political initiatives to introduce tax-deductible mortgages in Canada by Joe Clark at the federal level and Ernie Eves in the province of Ontario didn't fly. But now that it's clear that the policy for mortgage interest deduction has failed so miserably in the U.S., it's fairly safe to say that the issue is dead in Canada, and everywhere else in the world, for the foreseeable future.

It's easy to conclude that, as Canadian homeowners, we should take pride in our banking industry and housing market for being on very solid footing. We have avoided the universal financial system failure that afflicted the U.S. and much of the rest of the world, and perhaps we should feel somewhat relieved. We apparently dodged a bullet! Nevertheless, let's not pat ourselves on the back just yet. A truly successful long-term financial plan means being wealthy enough to choose retirement on your own schedule. That requires significant strategic planning around both your investments and your mortgage debt with effective tax planning at every stage of this lifelong process.

The good news is that the Canadian government looks favourably upon its investors and realizes that a bright economic future requires robust domestic investment in our economy from citizens and corporations alike. Our government happily awards tax breaks to Canadians who borrow to invest in the future of Canada, and it guarantees them by law. Some people worry that making their mortgage tax-deductible might somehow be viewed negatively by the government or that the CRA might become infuriated and begrudge having to honour a new tax deduction for an individual. This is utter nonsense! If you change your thinking and realize that engaging in a financial plan that proactively elevates you from a Canadian consumer to a Canadian investor, purely in the noble pursuit of funding your own personal retirement, your government will love you for it. You're a better Canadian citizen when you contribute positively to the economy through investment, and your entitlements, including tax benefits, are yours to enjoy or to reinvest as you see fit. Individual homeowners who proactively find a way to build wealth and fund their own futures are a blessing to this country, and your government should shake your hand and thank you as they hand back your hard-earned tax dollars every year.

Your journey to mortgage freedom is a noble quest for financial independence. As the Canadian mortgage debt swells from $1 trillion to $2 trillion over the next decade, nothing would be better for our fine country than if it were all tax-deductible, which means another much-needed $1 trillion would be invested in the Canadian economy.

Four Stages to Mortgage Freedom

You should view mortgage freedom as a lifelong journey that can span your entire adult working years. It starts on the day you purchase your first home and ends on the day you choose to retire—wealthy.

For the purpose of this book, the journey to mortgage freedom is divided into four distinct stages of mortgaged homeownership. Each of the four stages in the journey has its own mortgage strategy and investment objectives, as well as specific financial targets that are discrete and distinct from the other three stages. This is good news for all Canadians because it means that homeowners may begin their personal journey to mortgage freedom at any of the four stages described in this book.

Please note that the stages on your journey to mortgage freedom are progressive. While you don't necessarily have to complete each stage to advance to the next, you do need to meet the prerequisites of any stage before you can implement it.

The first stage begins when you decide to get in the game and purchase your first home. Generally speaking, the prerequisite for stage one includes sourcing adequate funds for your down payment and qualifying for your mortgage.

The second stage typically kicks in on the fifth anniversary of purchasing your home, when your mortgage comes up for the renewal. However, the true technical trigger (i.e. when you would first qualify for the second stage) is the point in time when you have paid down your mortgage enough to own 20% of the appraised value of your home. As soon as you have 20% equity in your home, you're ready to start the process of transferring your existing leverage to your retirement fund and start investing in your future.

The third stage is the most exciting, as it generates the

greatest financial benefit in the shortest period using the Tax Deductible Mortgage Plan (TDMP). You know you're ready for the third stage when you have built up substantial equity in your home above the initial 20% (typically another $100,000 or more). At this stage, you will begin paying off your mortgage in a rapidly accelerated manner using cash flow from investments created under the TDMP. This process will typically take between four and eight years and it will not require any cash from your own pocket beyond your regular mortgage payment.

For planning purposes, count on the TDMP to convert your mortgage into a tax-deductible investment loan in approximately one third of the remaining amortization period of your current mortgage (e.g. if your current mortgage has twenty-one years left in the amortization period, the accelerated TDMP will pay it off in less than seven years). The goal of the TDMP is to successfully transfer all your existing leverage from your home to your retirement fund so that you can start building greater wealth sooner, guaranteeing that you will have more money at retirement with less risk. In Canada, a key side benefit is that all your debt is now tax-deductible, which will save you hundreds of thousands of dollars in what would otherwise be unnecessary and wasteful contributions to the taxman!

At the end of third stage, your mortgage will be fully converted into a tax-deductible investment loan and your regular monthly payments of principal and interest will disappear, freeing up the cash flow that was committed to your monthly mortgage payment for other purposes, including investing or reducing tax-deductible debt.

The fourth stage is the home stretch! At this point in your life, mortgage freedom is yours! You have completed the TDMP and all your debt is tax-deductible. In this stage, you will evaluate your options on how to de-leverage your personal balance sheet and retire all your debt. You will learn how you can be your own banker by moving your debt into your RRSP. You then have to choose your final step on your journey to mortgage freedom. You should view the mortgage strategies detailed in the home stretch as your last chance to accelerate and achieve your retirement goals.

To help determine what stage you should be contemplating as your first step towards mortgage freedom, here is a summary of the four stages in the order they appear in the chapters that follow:

- Stage I: Get in the Game (First-Time Homebuyer)
- Stage II: Invest Early and Often (Cash Damming)
- Stage III: Hit the Gas! (Accelerate Your Plan)
- Stage IV: The Home Stretch (Be Your Own Banker)

Stage I: Get in the Game is for the first-time homebuyer. This will be your initial foray into homeownership and, in this section, we review the things you need to consider and understand as you get into the real estate market for the first time. Most Canadians complete their education and start working in their early twenties. The ambitious, frugal, and lucky among you will save enough money for a down payment on your first home before you're thirty years old, and your journey to mortgage freedom begins.

Stage II: Invest Early and Often is named after an old adage often ignored. In this stage, we introduce Canada's greatest invention since the telephone: the multi-component re-advanceable home equity line of credit (HELOC). A re-advanceable HELOC is a powerful tool for the individual Canadian taxpayer to reconstruct their balance sheet and implement superior financial plans that were all but impossible before now. Now that you understand why paying off your mortgage before you begin investing for retirement is such a poor financial strategy, Stage II is where you will learn how to tap into your home equity to become a responsible leveraged investor using small conservative monthly increments. Starting to invest in your retirement decades ahead of your neighbour who is on the more traditional path of paying off the mortgage first will give you the temporal diversification you need to build much greater wealth with no more risk.

Stage III: Hit the Gas! The Tax Deductible Mortgage Plan (TDMP) is an investment vehicle with laser-like focus: crush your mortgage out of existence in record time while building enough wealth for retirement on a schedule. In this stage, you will learn how to redirect the precious cash flow from your leveraged investments to eliminate your mortgage in one third of your current amortizing schedule. The key to Stage III is that you're never investing out of pocket! Converting all your mortgage debt into a tax-deductible investment loan is one of the wisest strategic moves you will ever make over the course of your working life and it will set you up to build the wealth you need to retire comfortably and avoid cost prohibitive options, such as reverse mortgages, in the future. You will learn how to convert your mortgage debt into tax-deductible investment debt by understanding the true value of building a non-registered portfolio of income-generating assets without using any of your own cash.

Stage IV: The Home Stretch happens after you have completed the TDMP and all your debt is 100% tax-deductible because it was transferred to support your retirement fund. This is the home stretch to a successful retirement and the objective is to be debt-free. In this stage, you will learn a strategy that you can implement to accelerate your wealth-building efforts, retire all your debt, and reach your long-term financial goals on time.

At each stage of this lifelong journey, there are steps you can take to improve your financial situation and accelerate your path to mortgage freedom. Whether you're currently contemplating purchasing your first home or are approaching retirement with your mortgage completely paid off, you can always proactively take action to optimize your financial situation and build wealth without using your own cash flow.

The typical wealth creation that you can generate through each stage of the mortgage freedom journey is detailed in its own section of the book, where the assumptions and time horizons are also discussed.

If you're just starting out today, you can reasonably expect to build great wealth through a forty-year journey to mortgage freedom. Similarly, if you're already in your forties and have owned a home for a decade or more, you can choose to jump right into the TDMP and maximize your efforts to build wealth for retirement over the ten or fifteen years you have left before you plan to stop working. Whatever stage of your journey you find yourself at currently, the mortgage and investment strategies described in this book will provide you with the opportunity to generate a material incremental financial benefit, and it's never too late to get started.

If you think that mortgage freedom sounds a bit like a promise of free money, you should realize that it's actually a simple retention plan to retain more of your own hard-earned dollars and keep mortgage interest payments in your own hands. When you consider that 80% or more of your gross income is going to the taxman and your mortgage banker, it can sometimes be too painful to keep a close eye on it or even to think about it too much. However, it's still your money—you must think about it and make plans to recover it. As a homeowner and investor, you need an active debt management plan that will ensure that the banks and the government don't "accidentally," or through neglect on your part, allow too much of your own hard-earned money to slip into their hands.

Some of you may think of mortgage freedom as a method of generating a substantial financial "bonus" by creating greater wealth for an earlier or more comfortable retirement. Others may look at mortgage freedom simply as a means to paying off your mortgage sooner. Regardless of your specific personal financial goal, mortgage freedom is a strategic roadmap that allows you to efficiently retain more of your income and invest it wisely for the long-term benefit of you and your family.

Good luck on *your* personal journey to mortgage freedom!

STAGE I
Get in the Game
(First-Time Homebuyer)

The Power of Leverage

The *Canadian Oxford Dictionary* defines *leverage* as "the mechanical advantage gained by use of a lever." In a general sense, you might think of the lever as the crowbar that moves the rock when you can't budge it with your bare hands. In a financial sense, *Oxford* also defines *leverage* as "[speculating] financially on borrowed capital expecting profits made to be greater than interest payable." This may be true, but in the context of homeownership, it's fair to think of leverage as simply the mortgage loan that allows you to buy the house that you couldn't otherwise afford.

Most people tend to think of their mortgage as a good thing before they get it and a bad thing every day thereafter. But how can a mortgage be a bad thing? After all, there are over twelve million homes in Canada, and five million of them are mortgaged. You now know that the total debt of Canadian homeowners reached $1 trillion for the first time in 2010. When you say "a trillion dollars" quickly, it might not sound like much. One trillion dollars, however, is a massive value. Just think of it for a moment. More than five million Canadian households have borrowed in excess of one thousand billion dollars ($1,000,000,000,000) to own their property. Now that is one big crowbar!

What If There Were No Mortgages?

Consider this. If there were no such thing as a mortgage, perhaps there would just be five million more renters in the world—five million poor souls who could never dream of homeownership. Property ownership in Canada would be a privilege of the elite! Like feudal landlords, only the very richest Canadians would own houses while the rest of us would rent from them.

Fortunately, our Canadian reality is quite different. As a nation, we pride ourselves in having one of the highest homeownership rates in the world thanks in large part to the concept of leverage and the existence of mortgages. Leveraged homeownership is the only thing that makes it possible for most of us. Think of it another way. At the time of purchasing your first home, what if there were no mortgages and you had to pay cash for it? Would this be possible? How much longer would it take you to get on the property ladder? Ten years? Fifteen years? Twenty? How many Canadians would wind up renting for the rest of their lives if there were no such thing as mortgages? Are you one of them? If so, perhaps you should think of your mortgage as your friend.

Well let's not get carried away. Your mortgage is not your friend. Certainly, your mortgage provided the leverage to achieve homeownership in the first place, but from the day you get one, it will be the single biggest drag on your financial success unless you manage it correctly.

The Biggest Crowbar: A High-Ratio Mortgage

When you get to the point in your life when you start to believe that renting a house isn't the right thing to be doing and you're ready to buy your first home, you will probably feel that your rent money is effectively cash being thrown away. You will be asking yourself why you're paying someone else's mortgage when you could be a homeowner paying your own mortgage and reaping the benefits down the road.

At this stage of your life, the key is to get in the game by becoming a homeowner as soon as is reasonably feasible. You know that you're finally ready to take the plunge into property ownership for the first time and can't wait to start shopping for your dream home. However, most Canadians at this stage of their life need the assistance of an independent mortgage professional. You understand that you will be better off in the long term if you own your own home, but you have no idea how to get started.

Professional Mortgage Advice

You should definitely consult an independent Accredited Mortgage Professional (AMP) to get reliable answers to questions about mortgages, especially if it's your first time buying a home. An AMP can provide you with free unbiased advice on exactly how much you can afford to spend on your home. Also, with your permission, an independent mortgage professional can access your credit report and pre-approve you for a mortgage at most lenders. The key benefit to an independent mortgage professional is that they have access to a broad range of lending institutions, as opposed to bank employees who are only allowed to promote the products of the bank that employs them. Consulting a mortgage professional and obtaining a full understanding of what you can afford and how big your mortgage can be before you start shopping for your home is an absolute no-brainer because it costs you nothing, commits you to nothing, and let's you know exactly how much you can afford to spend on a house.

In calculating how much you're going to be able to afford, there are two major financial considerations for the first-time homebuyer. The first is how much cash you can pull together for the down payment and closing costs, and the second is what you can afford as mortgage payments.

Mortgage Basics

You need to be able to comfortably afford your mortgage payments within your lifestyle regardless of what amount a lender pre-approves. Try to keep your total debt service (TDS) ratio under 40%, while keeping in mind that lower is always better. Your TDS measures all your living expenses and debt obligations against your gross income. Consult a mortgage professional who will do the detailed calculations for you, factoring in your down payment, mortgage insurance, closing costs, and credit and borrowing ratios so that you can be advised more accurately as to what you should budget to purchase your first home. After that, once you have picked out and purchased your home, you must make some decisions regarding term (floating or fixed interest rate) and amortization.

Term and Amortization

The term of your mortgage contract is different from the amortization period. The term refers to the term of your contract with the mortgage lender, which will be up for renewal at the end of the prescribed period. In Canada, most mortgage contracts are locked into a five-year term, but terms from six months to ten years are also available. If you select a five-year mortgage term, you have entered into a contract to make the mortgage payments for five years. At the end of that term, you will need to renew the mortgage with either your current lender or with another lender on new terms and interest rates that will reflect the prevailing rates at the time. It's vitally important to pay attention to your mortgage as it approaches the end of the term to give yourself enough time (e.g. at least four months) before your mortgage renewal date to speak with your mortgage professional, who will negotiate with lenders on your behalf and lock in new preferred terms at the then prevailing discount interest rates.

The amortization period is the length of time it will take you to pay off the mortgage in its entirety. The maximum amortization period for a Canadian mortgage is thirty-five years, unless the mortgage is high-ratio, in which case the maximum amortization period is thirty years.

Fixed or Variable Rate?

There are a few things that you should know before deciding between a fixed or variable interest rate. You can get reliable advice from your mortgage professional on whether to go fixed (i.e. lock in your interest rate for the duration of your mortgage term) or go variable (i.e. float the interest rate), as there is no material difference in the compensation paid by lenders to mortgage brokerages for placing you in a fixed or variable rate mortgage at the same term. They are paid the same either way. Knowing that your advisor doesn't make more money by influencing you one way or the other should give you some comfort that there is no financial bias.

You should understand the pros and cons of selecting a fixed or variable interest rate mortgage. In general, the advantage of a fixed rate is that your interest rate is known for the term of the mortgage, while the advantage of a variable rate (or adjustable rate) is that the interest rate is probably cheaper at the time you get the mortgage but will float throughout the term of your mortgage.

The other thing that should bring you comfort is that your lender doesn't really care whether you opt for a fixed rate or a variable rate mortgage, as they are guaranteed to make their money either way. Here's how that works.

Fixed rates are priced against the Government of Canada five-year benchmark bond yield, which fluctuates daily and is published by the government at www.bankof canada.ca/en/rates/bonds.html. Mortgage lenders will publish their five-year mortgage rates and will profit on the spread between the five-year bond, which is their cost of funds, and the five-year mortgage rate, which is what you will pay. As an example, if the five-year mortgage rate is 4% and the five-year benchmark bond yield is 2.5%, the lender has a 1.5% gross margin before expenses, being the spread between the cost of mortgage funds (2.5%) and the interest you, the borrower, pay (4%).

Variable rates, on the other hand, are priced against the prime rate, which will float with the overnight rate. In conducting monetary policy, the Bank of Canada meets eight times annually to set the overnight rate—the interest rate at which financial institutions may lend or borrow funds overnight to each other. As an example, if the overnight rate is 1%, then major financial institutions may set their prime rate at 3%. The spread can vary from 2% from time to time, but typically, all major financial institutions will have the same prime rate.

Over the last twenty years, homeowners with variable rate mortgages have done better (i.e. paid less interest) than those with fixed rate mortgages. This is largely because rates have trended down during this period. If you believe that interest rates are going to stay flat or trend further down, then variable is the way to go. On the other hand, if you believe that rates will rise over the term of your mortgage, then a fixed rate is preferable.

It's a personal choice. A key feature of a fixed rate is that it provides a certain level of security and comfort in knowing exactly what your interest payments will be over the term of your mortgage. A variable rate introduces risk in that you know your rate will move in lockstep with Canadian monetary policy as your lender adjusts their prime rate. In the grand scheme of things, in a stable interest rate environment with rates well below the historical average of 8%, it's not going to make a material difference.

One thing to keep in mind is that if you start out with a variable rate, you usually have the option to lock-in or switch to a fixed rate at any time. While this sounds like a great feature, the problem is that the privilege will be at the then prevailing fixed rates. This usually means that rates will have already risen by the time you realize you should have locked in. It will be a bit like closing the barn door after the horses have already left.

For first-time homebuyers in high-ratio mortgages in a time of record-breaking low interest rates, I would be very wary of gambling on a variable rate. A five-year fixed rate can provide some peace of mind. Again, the best person to advise you on this decision is your highly qualified independent AMP.

Planning Priorities for High-Ratio Borrowers

If you require a high-ratio mortgage to purchase your first home, your financial priorities from that day forth are simple. You must now start the process of de-leveraging until you reach the more comfortable conventional zone of around 4:1 debt-to-equity ratio, which can also be expressed as 80% loan-to-value (LTV). If you're young enough, there may not be anything wrong with having leverage at 9:1 (90% LTV) or 19:1 (95% LTV). The real risk is that being leveraged higher than 85% limits many of your options, including the option to refinance your mortgage loan with another lender. Under the new rules effective March 18,

2011, no borrower may refinance their mortgage until they have established at least 15% equity in their home. Therefore, while you are managing a high-ratio leverage loan, it's not yet the time to be actually investing for retirement. Simply put, you need to throw every spare nickel you have at your mortgage before doing anything else. Don't save. Don't invest in your RRSP. Don't spend.

There are two exceptions to this rule. The first is that you should make sure that you have access to emergency cash, and the second would be to pay off any other debts that carry a higher rate of interest before making an extra mortgage prepayment. You can gain access to emergency cash with an unsecured line of credit if you have one that you don't use. If you don't have an available line of credit or any other access to emergency cash, you need to create a source of liquid funds just in case of an unbudgeted problem. Systematically de-leveraging your home is a very good thing to do and is your second highest financial planning priority as a high-ratio borrower. But first, you need to be sure to establish access to a cash reserve as a safety net in case of emergency. Just remember, as you pay down that mortgage, it becomes your home equity and is completely illiquid.

An old adage says that the banks will only lend money to those who don't really need it. This may or may not be true, but the opposite is almost certainly true. The moment that an unforeseen event puts you into a financial bind that requires cash you don't have, you will almost certainly not qualify for the unsecured loan that you so desperately need. This is a particularly important consideration for those who borrow at 95% LTV with only 5% down, now that the new federal regulation prohibits you from refinancing your home until you have established a minimum of 15% equity. It would be a shame to be forced to sell your home because you need emergency access to cash and the only asset you have is the equity in your home. *If you don't yet have 15% equity in your home, it is imperative to establish your "rainy day fund" prior to making any discretionary prepayments on your mortgage.*

It's hard to imagine what our government was thinking when they implemented this disingenuous rule, but it's now a federal regulation, so it can't be ignored. Establishing an emergency line of credit or an emergency cash reserve is the only way that young Canadian homeowners with high-ratio mortgages can be sure they will not be forced to sell their home in the event they need quick access to cash.

Finance—How Much Can You Afford?

Before you start shopping, you need to consider a few things. The first thing that you need to do is figure out how much can you afford to spend on your home. The amount of cash you have saved for a down payment will be whatever you have in the bank or in other liquid non-registered investments. You cannot borrow your down payment, but if you have generous parents or other family members—and especially if your birthday is coming up—there is no better time in your life to ask for a generous cash gift than when you're trying to scrape together the down payment for your first home. In fact, if you need a good argument for Mom and Dad, it's probably fair to say that the more generous your parents are early on, by enabling their kids to get on the property ladder with their first home, the less of a liability you're likely to be to them in the future. Just remember, they can't loan you the money for a down payment on your home. There is no way around the rule against borrowing a down payment, so it must be a gift. Good luck with that!

RRSP—Home Buyers' Plan (HBP)

Before you go hat in hand to your parents for your down payment, however, you should make sure you have thoroughly exhausted your own resources. Another excellent source of cash for a down payment on your first home is your RRSP if you have one. The RRSP Home Buyers' Plan (HBP) is an outstanding government program that allows you to effectively use the money in your RRSP, without penalty, for this purpose. In effect, it's loaning money to yourself. You borrow the cash from your RRSP, interest-free, and repay it over the next fifteen years. There are a few rules for eligibility as follows:

- You have to be considered a first-time homebuyer. This condition can reset if you go five years without living in a home you own.
- If you have had a prior HBP loan, you must pay it off in the calendar year before re-engaging the HBP again.
- The maximum you are allowed to withdraw from your RRSP is $25,000 each.
- You have to actually buy or build a home that will be

your principal residence.

- You must make all withdrawals in the same calendar year.
- You have to file a T1036 form and file your tax return at year-end.

There are other rules and certain exceptions, but the HBP is generally a great source of cash for a first-time homebuyer. If your down payment (while accounting for closing costs) falls short of a full 20%, the HBP always makes good financial sense, as it saves on high-ratio mortgage insurance fees and will give you some much needed liquidity that will not be available again. In the event that you don't really need all the funds from your HBP, you can always use the excess cash to make a prepayment on your mortgage after it's funded. However, most first-time home buyers will find that they need all the cash that they can get their hands on to deal with moving costs and the expenses that go along with it. A key benefit of the HBP to these homeowners is that you don't actually have to start repaying it until the second year, which eases up your cash flow in the year you take possession of your new home.

Closing Costs and Related Expenses

The biggest mistake most first-time homebuyers make is not budgeting enough money for closing costs and moving expenses. As a rule, you should budget at least 2% of the property value for closing costs: legal fees, title insurance, land transfer tax, etc. The land transfer tax alone is going to cost you a bundle, so make sure you talk to your lawyer or mortgage professional and get a conservative estimate of what these fees will be.

Debt Servicing Ratios (GDS and TDS)

The second most important consideration in figuring out how much to spend on your first home is how much can you afford on mortgage payments. The standard for Canadian mortgages is to be amortized over twenty-five years. However, in recent years, longer amortizations of thirty-five years and longer have been approved by the federal government and supported by most lenders. The amortization period is key in determining how much mortgage you can afford. You will be making regular payments at least once every month for the foreseeable future, and you need to be confident that you can comfortably afford these payments. Your lender is going to help you with that by limiting the amount you can borrow based on your income and your other debt obligations. Once again, a good mortgage professional will be able to give you the exact number after reviewing your credit report.

As a general guideline, if your credit is excellent, you will be allowed to borrow up to a limit where your total monthly payments do not exceed a percentage of your income. This percentage or ratio is known as your total debt servicing ratio (TDS) and the upper limit for this ratio varies among lenders around the 40% mark plus or minus a few percentage points. The portion of total debt attributable to your mortgage, including taxes and heat, is known as your gross debt service ratio (GDS) and the upper limit for this ratio tends to be around 32%, although sometimes it can be waived altogether if your credit score is high enough. Of the five million mortgaged homes in Canada, approximately one third (1.5 million) are high ratio. Of these high-ratio mortgages, just 23% have a TDS greater than 40%, while 77% have less than 40%. The problem with being higher than 40% is that you will be house poor. Assuming that your only income is your salary, if 40% or more of your income goes to pay income and other taxes, and another 40% or more of your income goes to pay your mortgage, you can see the problem. You will be eating Kraft Dinner more often than not, and if you have kids of your own at this stage in your life, you will all eat Kraft Dinner all week long because that's all you'll be able to afford.

Insurance

When you purchase your first home, there are several different types of insurance that come into play, and it's important to understand each. First, there is life insurance. By taking on a mortgage, you have just taken on the largest debt of your life and you should complete a proper insurance review with a professional to ensure that appropriate coverage is in place to protect your family should something happen to you. These options include creditor life and term life insurance. The other type of insurance that will affect you if you're a high-ratio borrower (i.e. borrowing more than 80% of the value of the home) is mortgage insurance. This is the premium that you pay for the privilege of high leverage. The third type of insurance is title insurance. All of these various types of insurance are discussed below.

Creditor Life or Term Life Insurance

The purpose of insurance is to make sure that your family is looked after if something happens to you. Insurance isn't something that many people consider before they purchase a home, but as soon as you take on a mortgage, you should review your insurance needs with a professional.

There are two types of insurance to consider at this stage, both of which are intended to achieve the same goal. Creditor life insurance and term life insurance will reduce the risk to your family if you die by providing coverage that can pay off your mortgage debt.

Creditor life insurance is a convenient option that your mortgage professional will talk to you about at the time you arrange your loan. This coverage will assure that you're covered from the date you receive your mortgage funds, and it can be conveniently and easily tacked onto your mortgage. The important thing to know about creditor life insurance is that you don't designate the beneficiary, as the lender will be the beneficiary and the proceeds will pay off your mortgage directly.

A term life insurance policy has the clear benefit of designating the beneficiary so that your family has control of the money instead of your mortgage lender should something happen to you. Experts generally agree that meeting a licensed insurance professional to do a proper review of your insurance needs at the time you purchase your home is advisable. Very few mortgage professionals will also be life insurance experts, but some may have one in their office or be able to otherwise recommend one. Ask them.

If you're a first-time homebuyer with no insurance, it's recommended that you take the coverage offered to you by your mortgage professional and then arrange to see a licensed insurance expert to review your options and upgrade your coverage as appropriate. Many creditor life insurance policies will refund any premiums paid during the first thirty or sixty days. Remember, being underinsured as a new homeowner is an unnecessary risk, especially if you have dependents relying on you as the breadwinner.

Mortgage Insurance

The federal government determines the threshold for a high-ratio mortgage in Canada. It used to be 3:1, three parts mortgage to one part house. This means that you could get a conventional mortgage up to 75% of the appraised value of the property. Several years ago, the Minister of Finance raised the ratio to 4:1, easing the financial burden for new homeowners by increasing the conventional mortgage threshold to 80% of the value of a home and by reducing the insurance premium to be paid by those who needed more leverage than 80%.

Ideally, when you buy your first home, you want to have enough cash to make the 20% down payment in addition to funding the closing costs. If you don't have it, you will pay a minimum mortgage insurance premium for the additional leverage on a standard twenty-five-year amortizing loan of between 1.75% and 2.75% of the property value.

This insurance premium is a one-time fee that will be added to your mortgage balance when the deal closes, and the premium itself is not counted in the loan-to-value (LTV) ratio. The beneficiary of this insurance policy isn't you; it's the lender. You should consider this premium a cost of high leverage, and for that reason, make sure that you max it out in whatever band you're in. For example, if you absolutely need a mortgage amount of 91% or 92%, take the full 95% because you're paying for it anyway. After you have closed the deal and moved into your new home, you can always make a cash prepayment on the mortgage using any monies left over.

Title Insurance

Title insurance is a method of protecting lenders and homeowners against a future liability related to your property after you buy it. The typical kind of problems that can occur after you purchase your home range from an outstanding debt for unpaid property taxes by prior owners to legal claims against your title to the property for any number of reasons.

Title insurance is the domain of lawyers, not insurance brokers. You should speak to your lawyer about homeowner title insurance at the time you purchase your home. Many mortgage lenders require title insurance for their own benefit, and at your expense, as a condition of the mortgage loan. This is normal practice in Canada, but it's important to understand that lender title insurance protects only the lender and that you need homeowner title insurance to protect yourself. Some insurers offer dual policies at cost-effective pricing through lawyers. It's your real estate lawyer's obligation to advise you about title insurance and to arrange it on your behalf as a part of the closing process. Title insurance fees will be added to your legal bill and should be factored into closing costs when your purchase your home.

Look After Your Credit Score

Your credit score is critically important to your financial health. In Canada, the only circumstance in which a bank will lend you money is where they believe that you have the intent and the capability of making the prescribed loan payments. Canadian lenders insist on having genuine confidence in every borrower's ability to make their regular payments on their debt. There is no better way to gain such confidence than by looking at a borrower's history of making past loan payments and reviewing borrowing habits and patterns.

As a mortgaged homeowner, it's important for you to understand that your debts and your behaviour in making payments are tracked very carefully at every turn, and no lender would ever consider providing you with a loan until they have completed a satisfactory review of your credit history. While your mortgage itself may not be reported to the credit bureaus, most of your other debts are. If you have never reviewed your own credit history, it's probably safe to say that you will be astonished at the level of detail that is readily available to any financial institution or lender when you grant them permission to review it. Many people mistakenly believe that the better their credit score, the lower their interest rate. This isn't necessarily true. In Canada, there is a magic threshold of creditworthiness where you're considered likely to pay your debts, and if you don't meet it, you will simply not be deemed worth the risk. This threshold is summed up by a single number: your credit score. In the Canadian mortgage industry, this is sometimes referred to as your Beacon score.

History of Credit Scoring

In the old days, getting a mortgage meant visiting your local bank branch to meet with the branch manager. You would sit across the desk and make your case for homeownership, carefully explaining how you came up with your down payment and why you would be a good bet for repaying the loan. The manager would inquire about your employment and bill payment history, and perhaps would review your banking history. After sizing you up, he (typically) would make a decision about you, and if all went well, you would leave with a commitment in hand and ready to shop for your first home. There would be little discussion if any about interest rates because you would be happy to simply accept what was offered. Times have changed!

Today, you can still meet with your branch manager, along with a myriad of financial experts and mortgage specialists. You can even visit them online from the comfort of your home. Indeed, everyone seems to be clamoring to get their hands on a loan application from you, but their gut feeling no longer matters. More than ever, a three-digit number will decide whether you're a good or bad bet. That number is your credit score, and understanding how it works and what you can do to improve it is one of the most important things you can do for your financial health.

Credit scoring is not a new concept for banks and credit companies. Most have deployed some in-house version of credit prediction formulas for decades, usually applied on an individual basis by loan officers. The U.S.-based Fair Isaac Corporation, an industry pioneer, created their widely adopted credit scoring formulas in the mid-'50s, and by the mid-'80s, they began applying the formulas against the huge amounts of data held by the major credit bureaus. The result was the FICO score, and it was such a successful predictor of creditworthiness that in 1995, the two biggest U.S.-based mortgage finance agencies, Freddie Mac and Fannie Mae, recommended U.S. lenders adopt the FICO score in mortgage underwriting. This helped ignite an explosion in consumer credit in the U.S. (and Canada), and the result is that your credit score has now become the defining feature of your borrowing power.

The first thing to understand about your credit score is that you don't have one, but two. The two major credit bureaus in Canada, Equifax and TransUnion, track loan payment behaviour of millions of Canadians and use this data to score each individual. Equifax produces a Beacon score, a variation of the U.S. FICO score, and generates a value within the 300 to 900 range. TransUnion produces their own credit score with a range of 300 to 850. Most people score in the 650 to 799 range. If you score above 700, it should be easy for you to qualify for loans and low interest rates. However, if your score is lower than the magic number established by the lender as the threshold of creditworthiness, good luck trying to get a cell phone, let alone a credit card, car loan, or mortgage.

So, if credit scores are so important, why are so many Canadians in the dark about what they are and how they work? The main reason is that the scores were never intended to be used by consumers. They were a tool provided to banks, insurers, and credit companies to predict consumer behaviour. In addition, they are based on proprietary formulas owned by the credit-scoring companies who aim to protect their intellectual property not only from each other but also from consumers who might try to beat the systems if they know too much about how they work.

It wasn't until early 2000 that outcries for transparency from consumer advocate groups resulted in legislation that forced credit-scoring companies to draw back the curtain, at least to a certain extent, and show us how their systems worked. The result is that while the industry still harbours a substantial amount of secrecy, consumers now have a better understanding around how scores are calculated and what they can do to improve them.

What's Your Credit Score?

There are essentially five criteria at work in generating a credit score:

1. *Payment history.* This accounts for about 35% of your score and analyzes your past bill paying behaviour. Have you ever missed a payment? If so, how many payments have you missed in a row? Do you carry balances month over month or do you diligently pay your cards off? Like many aspects of life, an analysis of your past behaviour predicts your future behaviour, so this is the most heavily weighted section of your score.

2. *Current level of indebtedness.* This section makes up about 30% of your score and looks at the total amount of credit granted to you and how you use it. What are the limits on your credit cards or lines of credit? How

close are your balances to these limits? Do you have a wallet full of credit cards? Do you carry no cards at all? As the second most heavily weighted section, the objective here is to determine what type of credit user you are by analyzing how you use the credit you have already been granted.

3. *Length of credit history*. This section is worth about 15% of your score and either rewards or punishes you for the length of time you have been a credit user. It's not necessary to have used credit for a long time to generate a good score, but generally speaking, the longer your credit history, the better your score will be.

4. *Number and frequency of new credit enquiries*. This section accounts for about 10% of your score and highlights the complexity of the formulas when attempting to correctly categorize consumer behaviour. Are you a person constantly looking to build reserves of credit? This credit-seeking behaviour can indicate looming financial trouble that could increase risk to the lender. On the other hand, shopping around for the best rates on mortgages or auto financing is considered prudent consumer behaviour. In such cases, multiple enquiries submitted from mortgage or auto companies within a two-week period are counted as one enquiry when formulating your score.

5. *Types of credit*. This section is also weighted to about 10% of your score. It attempts to assess not only your

ability to manage different types of debt but how susceptible you are to overloading yourself. The two main types of debt are revolving (credit cards, lines of credit, etc.) and installment (mortgages, auto loans, personal loans, etc.). Carrying both types of credit is generally viewed as positive, but carrying too many of one or both types is usually a negative.

Now that we know how credit bureaus generate your score, you need to understand how you can improve it. Credit scores are not static. Your score is constantly re-evaluated every time data is passed from credit companies to the credit bureaus, often monthly. This is both a good and bad thing. If your score drops below the threshold of creditworthiness because you neglected to make a credit card payment in July, you might find yourself unable to qualify for a mortgage in August. On the plus side, if you have just come through a rough patch and are looking to clean up your credit and improve your score, the right behaviour will also be rewarded in due course.

Improving Your Credit Score

There are five ways to improve your credit score:

1. *Know your credit score and profile.* As they say: we don't do better until we know better. After all, how can you fix something unless you know it's broken? Regularly obtaining a copy of your credit report is both a good habit and an excellent way to check up on your credit profile and avoid becoming a victim of identity

theft. You can request an online copy of your credit report from Equifax or TransUnion for $14.95 at the time of this publication. You can even receive a free copy, provided you make the request in writing and have it mailed to you. In either case, if you want to also see your credit score, you will be charged a small fee of $7.95 to $9.95 respectively. The good news is that requesting your own credit report and score has no impact whatsoever on your credit score.

If you find inaccuracies on your credit report, you should act fast to get them corrected. You have the option of contacting the credit bureau directly, but the fastest approach is to contact the financial institution, since that's where the error originated. Errors should be corrected within thirty days. If not, follow up with the complaints department of your financial institution.

2. *Pay your bills on time.* This should be obvious, but there are many who think that being just a few days or a few weeks late won't have much of an impact. They're wrong! Late payments have the largest negative impact on your score and payments late by more than ninety days can damage your score for many years, just like bankruptcy and collections.

Credit bureaus assign a number to loan payments using a graded system from 1 to 9, where 1 means you always pay on time and 9 means you don't pay at all. Many lenders, especially mortgage lenders, have internal policies that limit the number or severity of late payments before declining a loan application outright.

Don't let the calendar run you over. Most online banking systems provide a free recurring bill payment feature. Find out when your bills are due each month and set up a recurring payment so you don't have to think about when bills are due. Also, keep in mind that more and more companies report to credit bureaus, including some cell phone carriers, and it's probably only a matter of time before all utility companies follow suit. Take advantage of online systems and you will never fall behind in payments.

3. *Manage your debt.* The best way to manage your debt is to pay it off every month. This will save you a fortune in interest payments, but it will also pretty much ensure you maintain a consistently high credit score. Carrying no balances may be something we all aspire to, but it's simply not a reality for many people. The next best thing we can do is look at how best to manage outstanding balances. Some people might find it convenient to use only one card or concentrate spending on a single card to collect the rewards points it offers. The trick here is to make sure you aren't building rewards points at the expense of your credit score. You should always avoid reaching a balance of more than 70% of the available limit. Once you reach this amount, use a different card to handle excess credit requirements.

Of course, this doesn't mean that you should open additional credit accounts just because you're running high balances. Managing debt ultimately means paying off debt, and if your debt is continually rising, you might need to consider a lifestyle change of avoiding debt altogether rather than just swapping balances around different cards.

4. *Build a credit history.* Demonstrating a long history of paying your bills on time and managing your credit responsibly is the best way to maintain a good credit score and repair broken credit. As the saying goes, time heals all wounds. You should think of bad credit as a financial injury that will take some time to nurse back to health. However, there are some things to keep in mind along the way.

   A trap that people often fall into when trying to repair damaged credit is believing it to be in their interest to close credit cards or other accounts. In fact, closing credit that has already been granted is unlikely to help improve your score and could have quite the opposite effect. Closing accounts that have been active for a long time can make your credit history look a lot younger than it is. Closing accounts also means you have less available credit, which means balances you're carrying will have a relatively heavier impact on your score. The better approach is to keep everything as it is and simply pay balances off. Also, find out which accounts are the oldest and ensure you run minimal transactions through them each month, paying them in full if possible. This will improve your score in the shortest time possible by demonstrating your longstanding credit management skills.

5. *Avoid excessive credit enquiries.* Every time you make a loan application, whether for a revolving loan such as a credit card or an installment loan such as a mortgage, a credit inquiry is made against you. With every inquiry, your credit score drops a little bit (in keeping with the rules discussed earlier for multiple auto or mortgage requests within a short time frame). This means that you shouldn't apply for credit you don't need. Lenders become wary when they see you stockpiling credit because it might appear that you are taking on an unmanageable debt load. Once you have a reasonable mix of revolving and installment loans and a credit score in the range of 700, resist the urge to pile more on. It won't help you.

But what if you don't have a credit score at all? It might seem like a Catch-22. You need a credit history to get credit, but you can't get credit without a credit history. To a certain extent, it's true, but there are some tricks that can help you establish a credit score for the first time or rebuild one that has been destroyed and not simply damaged (bankruptcy, especially as a result of divorce, tends to have this effect).

One of the best credit-building strategies is to use secured credit cards. These are essentially prepaid credit cards that can quickly and effectively start or rebuild your credit history. Best of all, you only need about $500 (sometimes less) to get started. Simply purchase a secured credit card and use the card regularly, running it up to no more than 70% of the available limit each month. Pay it off in full each month if you can, but at least make regular payments on time. It's that simple.

Another way to establish or rebuild your credit score is to hitch yourself to someone already established and piggyback on their good record. Open a joint account and take on the payments. Of course, this requires that you know someone with an impeccable credit history willing to let you ride along.

By following the above steps and managing your credit responsibly, your score should remain well above the 700 range. As a result, your independent mortgage professional will be able to offer you the best rates available when you need them. Just remember that your credit score is a constantly changing number and you need to be diligent in maintaining it so it doesn't let you down when you need it the most!

STAGE II
Invest Early and Often
(Cash Damming)

Congratulations! You've just graduated into a whole new class of homeownership: the conventional borrower. When you were a high-ratio borrower, you had no real opportunity to consider any kind of discretionary investments because paying down your mortgage and building equity in your home was your single overriding financial priority. Now that you have effectively de-leveraged your home to the conventional zone (i.e. under 80%, or less than a 4:1 debt-to-equity ratio), you're ready to start looking at investment options and to making your mortgage tax-deductible.

Although some homeowners will follow a cautious path and pay off their mortgage before starting to invest, the majority of Canadian homeowners will simply not wait twenty or thirty years before becoming an investor. Whether you borrow to start a small business, for a down payment on an investment property, or to invest in the market to build your retirement fund, the reality is that active debt management is a more tax-efficient approach from the moment you begin to invest.

The primary purpose of any investment should be to make a profit, and as long as the investment has the capability of paying income to the investor, a holistic approach to debt management becomes the only sensible approach to managing your finances. While the most predictable and reliable benefit will usually be related to deferred taxes, there are other significant financial benefits as well.

Now that you have effectively de-leveraged your home into the conventional zone, it's possible to start accessing the equity in your home in small increments every month to build your retirement portfolio. It's this process that forms the foundation for bulking up your retirement funds safely and creating a larger nest egg for the future without using your own cash. Time is on your side. The book *Lifestyle Investing* provides the evidence that borrowing to invest at this stage of your life is the least risky approach to building the nest egg you will need in the future.

In this section, we will explore the financial benefits of proper debt management in the context of the various categories of investors.

What Kind of Investor Are You?

Mortgage Freedom contains a sound strategy for all types of income-seeking investors. It's not an objective of this book to opine the merits of any one type of income-generating investment over another, but rather to educate you on how to properly structure your debt in support of the personal investment choices you will elect to make during each stage of your personal journey to mortgage freedom. There's no guarantee that author bias won't creep in from time to time. The goal of this book is to ensure that all homeowners who have already decided to become some form of income investor, before they have fully paid off their mortgage, have an appropriate debt-management strategy in place and a sound strategic plan to optimize their tax benefits along the way.

There are several types of qualified Canadian investors ranging from those who own their own business to those who own the business of others (through the public markets), to government or corporate debt (bondholders), real estate debt (mortgagees), and real estate property investors—to name but a few. While these investments may appear quite different in nature, they all have one thing in common: each is capable of generating income and our federal watchdog, the Canada Revenue Agency (CRA), is compelled to allow the tax deductibility of interest on any money that was specifically borrowed for the purpose of making such investments.

There are significant advantages in proactively engaging a long-term debt-management strategy when some of your debt, especially your mortgage debt, isn't tax-deductible. You should no longer simply wait until your five-year mortgage term is up for renewal before considering your options! You need to start planning today. Now is the time to upgrade your personal mortgage strategy by seeking professional guidance on a long-term debt plan that will complement and accelerate your investment efforts. Do this and you will sleep better at night in the full confidence that you're doing the very best to build a wealthy future for you and your family.

Shooting the Sacred Cow

As mentioned above, Canadians have no issues when it comes to borrowing to purchase their home but think differently about borrowing to build a nest egg.

Somehow, it appears as if we have been conditioned to believe that it's better to invest our savings while borrowing to buy stuff such as cars and big-screen TVs. This problem stems from the lack of personal finance education in our public school systems. Ignorance about basic personal finance is damaging the balance sheets of many Canadian families and hindering their wealth-building efforts. So how do we learn when there is no lesson plan at school? For many Canadians, the personal lessons come from our parents. More's the pity.

Conventional Canadian tradition would have you *save your money while borrowing to spend*. When you consider that the biggest single expense in your life is your home, if you could leave emotion and tradition out of it, you would definitely have to question the wisdom of this type of thinking.

Canadian tax planning advantages alone dictate that it makes much more sense to *spend your money and borrow to invest*. If you are a tax accountant or a qualified financial advisor, you know that borrowing to invest while spending your own cash on consumer goods is the superior approach to personal finance.

If you take only one lesson from this book, it should be

this: *spend your money and borrow to invest.* It might seem counterintuitive at first, and it's certainly contrary to traditional beliefs, but the rationale behind this superior approach to managing your personal finances will become clear in due course. You will become richer simply by changing your behaviour as an investor.

Good Debt versus Bad Debt

One reason why you want to spend your own money while borrowing to invest is the two types of debt: good debt and bad debt. There is only one simple difference between good debt and bad debt and that is whether the interest on the debt is tax-deductible. This confuses many people, as there are many common uses of the terms *good debt* and *bad debt*, and they all have their own various definitions. The traditional belief of many families is that *all* debt is bad and that we should attempt to be debt-free. This fallacy isn't helpful when it comes to building a secure retirement and achieving mortgage freedom.

The online information available to ordinary Canadians who are trying to learn about their personal finances is confusing, contradictory, and often completely erroneous. Some would have you believe that it's impossible to have a tax-deductible mortgage on your home or that an investment loan is always going to be tax-deductible. Neither of these statements is true. The fact is that some investment loans may not be tax-deductible or may lose their tax-deductible status over time. Likewise, the loan on your home, your principal residence, may very well be fully tax-deductible or may become tax-deductible over time.

First, the legal structure of the security used for any debt is of absolutely no consequence in determining whether a loan is good debt or bad debt. It's simply irrelevant to the issue of tax deductibility whether the security for a debt is legally registered as a collateral charge or a standard charge mortgage. Whether you use your principal residence or an investment property to secure a loan has no relevance as to whether it's good debt or bad debt. Nor does it matter how the repayment of the debt is structured. For example, whether a debt has interest-only payments forever or is paid off monthly on an amortizing schedule of principal and interest over twenty-five or thirty-five years has nothing to do with whether it's good debt or bad debt. All of these types of securities, legal instruments, and payment structures are common in Canada, and any combination can be classified as either good debt or bad debt for the purpose of interest deductibility. Contrary to common belief, the mortgage on your Canadian principal residence could very well be tax-deductible (good debt) depending only on what you use the money for.

For clarity, the only factor you should consider in determining whether a loan is going to be classified as good debt or bad debt is what you do with the cash. Specifically, at the time you take out the loan, you must ask yourself what you actually did with the money. Canadians generally believe that their mortgage isn't tax-deductible, and that is often the case. This is because the mortgage was taken out to actually buy the home in the first place.

Unlike in the U.S., a Canadian home doesn't qualify as an investment for loan-interest tax deductibility under CRA rules because you live there. When you live there, you can't charge yourself rent; therefore, your principal residence, or any other home that you don't rent out, has no capacity to generate income and will always be considered bad debt by the CRA. On the other hand, if you had purchased the same property with the same mortgage with different intentions, you could consider the mortgage good debt. Specifically, if you purchase a property with the intent to rent it out to someone else, the mortgage interest is tax-deductible, and this is the case even if you secure the mortgage with your principal residence.

Bad-Debt Mortgage

In Canada, you cannot consider yourself a leveraged investor when you take out a mortgage to buy your own home. To be a leveraged investor, where the loan interest would be tax-deductible, you must borrow money to purchase assets that have the capacity to generate income. You might feel like your home is an investment, but our federal government disagrees. Your principal residence doesn't meet the CRA test for eligible investments, where the interest on money borrowed to acquire them would be tax-deductible, even though you may personally consider the purchase of your home to be the best investment you've ever made!

One of the key objectives of this book is to show you how to transform yourself from being a highly leveraged homeowner into a leveraged investor to benefit from the significant financial and tax benefits you can reinvest to achieve mortgage freedom. The leverage you take on initially to become a homeowner stops serving its purpose the day you own the home. From that day forward, you should systematically transfer it towards the noble goal of building your retirement. This is the key message when you understand the benefit of financing your retirement like you financed your home.

Understanding the distinction between being a leveraged homeowner and a leveraged investor is critical. As a borrower, you took on a necessary debt to make the transition from renter to owner because you had no other choice. The mortgage debt was required because you didn't have enough money to buy your home in cash, and since the asset you purchased didn't qualify as an investment under the Income Tax Act, the interest on your mortgage isn't tax-deductible.

Taking out a mortgage to buy your home may have been a necessary debt taken on for good reasons, but it's all bad debt.

Make Your Mortgage Tax-Deductible

Making a mortgage tax-deductible is *not* a new financial strategy. Enshrined in the Canadian Income Tax Act section 20 (1) (c) for over ninety years is the fundamental rule that if a taxpayer borrows money to invest in an asset that has the capability of paying income, the interest is tax-deductible.

Historically, Canadian homeowners had very little choice when it came to selecting a mortgage or implementing a mortgage strategy. Standard charge terms for mortgages varied little and consumers were simply required to select a term and opt for a fixed or variable interest rate. The recent proliferation of multi-component re-advanceable HELOC products in the Canadian market has resulted in the general public becoming increasingly aware that they have options to restructure their mortgage for tax benefits.

A group that makes up less than 10% of the population owns over 50% of the property in this country. We refer to these landowners as the wealthy, and they separate themselves from ordinary homeowners in that their mortgages are already 100% tax-deductible. It's important to know that tax benefits enjoyed by the wealthy are not due to a loophole in the Income Tax Act, nor are these tax benefits based on any tax rule that is likely to be changed. If the government were to attempt to change the fundamental principle that our economy was built on—that if you borrow money to invest in this country, the interest is tax-deductible—there would be a riot on Bay Street. Every Canadian entrepreneur needs to borrow money when they start a business, and if the interest weren't tax-deductible, it would greatly increase the likelihood of business failure.

Debt Conversion Is the Key!

Wealthy Canadians employ professional accountants who understand these tax rules and have been using this knowledge to their financial benefit for almost 100 years. As an example, if you, as an individual, happened to be wealthy with enough liquid assets to pay off your mortgage entirely (e.g. even if you had to sell some unregistered investments), you could own your own home, free and clear from a mortgage. You wouldn't need a strategy to slowly transfer your leverage from your home to your retirement fund systematically over time because you could do it all in one day and proceed directly to the last stage of your journey to mortgage freedom (Stage IV).

If you were wealthy, you would first use your available cash to pay off and then discharge your existing mortgage and then arrange a new investment line of credit on your home and buy back any investments you sold to pay off the mortgage in the first place. Your new line of credit would be 100% tax-deductible, assuming only that your investments had the capacity to generate income or were otherwise qualified under CRA rules. This technique is often referred to as a direct debt swap and is also known as the "Singleton Shuffle," named after the Vancouver lawyer John Singleton, who famously won his Canadian Supreme Court case in 2001. This case is discussed in more detail later in the Appendix.

In reality, most ordinary mortgaged Canadian homeowners don't have a few hundred thousand dollars kicking around to buy a home outright. You will need the proceeds from your mortgage to buy your home unless you happen to win a lottery the day before. Since the CRA doesn't consider the purchase of your principal residence as an eligible investment, your mortgage is bad debt, as it isn't tax-deductible. You will therefore need to set up a CRA-approved cash-damming process to transform your bad-debt mortgage into an investment line of credit.

The cash-damming mortgage strategy is specifically geared for qualified homeowners who are interested in improved tax efficiency, paying off the mortgage sooner, and generating greater wealth for retirement with acceptable risk.

Cash Damming

The Canadian Income Tax Act section 20 (1) (c) provides that interest charged on money borrowed to invest for the purpose of generating income is tax-deductible. Therefore, if you borrow money to purchase an income-generating investment (e.g. mutual funds), the interest expense from the loan is tax-deductible regardless of where you borrowed the money or what security you used for the loan.

Cash damming is a term the CRA first defined in an interpretation bulletin IT-533, published on October 31, 2003, to help individual taxpayers determine under what circumstances interest would be tax-deductible. Paragraph 16 of IT-533 introduces cash damming as follows:

> Taxpayers may segregate (typically in separate accounts) funds received from borrowed money and funds received from other sources (e.g. funds received from operations or other sources and that are otherwise not linked to money previously borrowed). This technique, commonly referred to as cash damming, readily allows taxpayers to trace borrowed money to specific uses.

The greatest invention in the mortgage industry is the latest form of home equity line of credit (HELOC). Don't confuse this with the traditional revolving line of credit, which is characterized by a single debt component and interest-only payments. This revolutionary product is a multi-component re-advanceable HELOC that provides you with great flexibility as well as the opportunity to efficiently implement the technique referred to as cash damming.

Home Equity Line of Credit (HELOC)

The first major advantage of a multi-component HELOC is the flexibility of a single loan to be carved up into multiple independent debt components that will each track and report principal balances and interest payments separately. Each component may have its own fixed or variable interest rate, amortizing period, or be a non-amortizing or purely revolving component. Another key feature of the multi-component HELOC is its versatility to automatically re-advance monies paid back to the original amount. By being both multi-component and re-advanceable, a HELOC is a far superior loan product to a regular mortgage with standard charge terms.

The multi-component nature of the HELOC is the manner in which we are able to segregate tax-deductible debt from non-tax-deductible debt in the cash dam and it's the reason why we can be confident that we don't intermingle the two different types of debt. The two components of a HELOC work in tandem—when you pay down the principal in the amortizing bad-debt *mortgage* component, it's added back to the good-debt *line of credit* component. This brings the original HELOC available balance back to the original approved balance every time you make a payment.

The ability to immediately borrow back every dollar of principal as you pay down your mortgage is the key feature that these new HELOC products have to offer. In the past, anytime you wanted to get money back out of your mortgage, you would have to break the current mortgage and take out a new one, which would be cost prohibitive and administratively onerous. A new multi-component HELOC is designed to automatically free up smaller contributions for monthly investing, which puts the power of compound interest squarely into your hands.

The re-advanceable feature of the HELOC is necessary to optimize the financial benefits and maximize your annual tax refunds. It's the underpinning feature that makes cash damming both viable and well worth the effort. The HELOC will be re-advanceable to the original approved loan amount and can be drawn down automatically in the line of credit as the amortizing component is paid off. Lenders who offer the specific type of HELOCs that meet these stringent requirements for both re-advanceability and multiple components that work in tandem are listed on the *Mortgage Freedom* website at www.mortgagefreedom.ca.

If you own your home free and clear and are taking out a new mortgage to invest in its entirety, then your mortgage interest will be 100% tax-deductible. Cash damming isn't required, and the structure of the mortgage is irrelevant.

The Collateral Charge Advantage

In Canada, the HELOC is a relatively new type of secured debt on residential property. It has a different legal structure than a conventional mortgage and is legally registered as a collateral charge instead of a normal mortgage standard charge. A HELOC isn't really a mortgage at all; it's a revolving line of credit that just happens to contain components that quack like a mortgage, including an amortizing period with regular payments of principal and interest.

For example, you can visit your independent mortgage professional, who can arrange a $300,000, multi-component re-advaceable HELOC that contains a $250,000 "mortgage" component that amortizes over twenty-five years in addition to a $50,000 revolving line of credit that can be set to automatically re-advance as the mortgage component is paid off. Instead of a $250,000 mortgage, you now have a $300,000 HELOC that contains a component that looks and behaves like a $250,000 mortgage in every way. The difference is that you now also have a separate $50,000 line of credit component that will increase every month as you pay off the mortgage principal. If the mortgage payment is $1,500, of which $425 is principal and $1,075 is interest, after the first payment, the HELOC balance will remain at $300,000, with a $249,575 amortizing mortgage balance and a $50,425 line-of-credit balance. The flexibility comes with the use of the line of credit. If you don't draw it down, it remains unused and you won't pay any interest on it. If you do draw it down and invest the proceeds properly, the interest on the line of credit will be tax-deductible.

The creation of the multi-component re-advanceable HELOC means that there are now two types of mortgages in Canada. Historically, mortgages have been traditionally registered as what is legally referred to as a "conventional charge" against the property. A conventional charge is a legal instrument in which all the terms of the mortgage, including the amortization schedule and interest rate, are defined. The introduction of the HELOC as a flexible alternative to the traditional mortgage has mandated a different method of registering the lender's security. The security for a HELOC is in effect a promissory note with a lien against the property, or what is legally referred to as a "collateral charge."

Although a HELOC provides great flexibility, there are pros and cons to the homeowner with respect to securing their home loan with a collateral charge versus a conventional charge. You can re-advance a collateral charge up to the original amount borrowed; however, a mortgage amortizes on a schedule and you may not re-advance the principal balance after you have paid it down, as it is a conventional charge. A HELOC registered as a collateral charge may be registered in a different amount than the amount authorized to be advanced to the borrower and the amount advanced can actually be increased at a future date without having to reregister the security. This would have to happen at the request of the borrower and with the approval of the lender and would typically be granted when either the home value or the borrower's capacity to handle more debt increases.

For example, a HELOC may be registered at 100% or 125% of the appraised value of the property, while only 80% of the value of the property may actually be available to the borrower. The advantage of this over-collateralization to the borrower is that if the property value increases, the qualified borrower may be able to increase the limit on their HELOC to 80% of the newly appraised value without having to refinance the loan and pay the legal fees associated with the discharge of the existing mortgage and registration of a new one.

There are other advantages related to being able to carve

up the HELOC into multiple components that have their own separate terms, rates, and amortization schedules. These advantages relate to the specific financial strategies described in each stage of this book. However, there are also disadvantages. One disadvantage to a borrower is that a collateral charge isn't routinely transferred between lenders, so if a borrower wants to switch lenders at the end of a mortgage term, they would incur additional legal expenses that they wouldn't have been required to pay when simply switching a conventional mortgage to a new lender. Also, if a HELOC is over-collateralized by having the registered value exceed the amount of the actual loan, it would likely restrict the borrower's ability to get a second mortgage on the same property, as the security available to a lender in the second position would be diminished.

While the consumer continues to have the choice of whether to get a conventional mortgage registered as a conventional charge or a HELOC registered as a collateral charge, the trend is unmistakeably moving in the direction of universal collateral charges. If there were any doubt about this trend, it was put to rest in 2010 when the first of Canada's tier-one chartered banks announced that it would begin to register 100% of all loans secured by residential property as collateral charges. Regardless of whether the borrower wants a regular mortgage or a HELOC, the registration will be a collateral charge registered at up to 125% of the property value at the homeowner's discretion. This is an interesting move, as it's likely indicative of the general migration towards flexible lines of credit over conventional amortizing mortgages in Canada. Canadian borrowers can reasonably expect this migration towards collateral charges in favour of conventional charges to continue in the years to come, especially as other mortgage lenders in Canada follow the leader and phase out conventional charges.

How Cash Damming Works

Before you setup a cash dam, you will probably need to refinance your current mortgage. It's strongly recommended that you use the services of an independent mortgage professional or a TDMP Certified Mortgage Planner (a list can be found at www.mortgagefreedom.ca). If you have a properly structured HELOC set up, you can establish a CRA-approved cash dam as described in the following diagram:

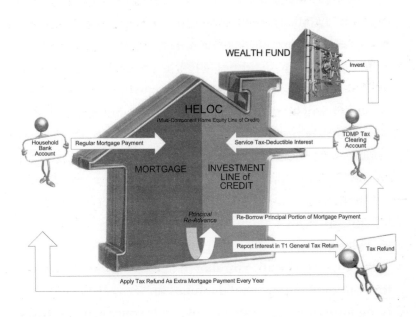

In the diagram, you will see that your household debt is divided into two components. On the left side, you have the amortizing mortgage component, which is a regular amortizing mortgage that will replace your existing bad mortgage debt and any other consumer debt that you may have had, including credit card debt. On the right side, there is the line-of-credit component, which has been named the investment line of credit (ILOC). In this new multi-component HELOC structure, the ILOC is re-advanceable, and as you pay down the principal on the left side, the amount paid will automatically be added to the ILOC.

Professional advice from a financial advisor whose job it is to ensure that your investments meet the CRA's guidelines, and a tax accountant familiar with cash damming, will assure your entitlement to your tax refunds.

Here is how it works. To use a simple example in the context of the diagram, the cash-damming process starts with your regular mortgage payment, which we will assume to be $1,000, consisting of $400 in principal and $600 in interest. As soon as you make this payment, your amortizing mortgage will be paid down by $400 and your HELOC will automatically re-advance a matching amount (i.e. the $400 principal payment) into the ILOC component on the right side of the diagram.

In the cash dam, the $400 principal payment will be automatically drawn down from your ILOC into a dedicated, special purpose, no fee, chequing account, which is shown in the above diagram. You should open a chequing account for your cash dam so that the funds are invested in a qualifying investment, as agreed upon with your financial advisor, and this will typically be achieved through a monthly recurring automated process known as a pre-authorized cheque (PAC). The CRA prescribes that cash damming should be conducted in separate accounts, and that is why it's recommended that you open a dedicated account for this purpose and ensure that you don't mix other personal funds in the same bank account.

If you wish to have your cash dam be self-funding so that you do not need to make any additional monthly payments (other than your mortgage payments), you will need to set up the monthly PAC to only invest a portion of the $400 that is available. This leaves a suitable amount of money held back in your no-fee chequing account to pay the interest on the ILOC. In the above example, although $400 has been cash dammed to a bank account, perhaps only $380 will be re-invested, which would leave $20 as a holdback to cover the interest on the ILOC. For cash flow planning, it's worth noting that some lenders require a minimum payment of up to $50 even though the actual interest component may be very small. In this case, the portion of the payment that is not interest will be applied to principal and will be drawn down again in the following month.

Making the interest payment from your new bank account on the right side of the diagram is an important element of a proper cash-dam setup because it serves two key objectives. First, it's tax efficient. Under Canadian tax rules, the interest on money borrowed to pay the interest on a loan that is tax-deductible is also tax-deductible. Second, since your new bank account pays this interest, your cash dam is self-funding and you therefore don't have to fund the interest from your own financial resources.

You will, of course, always be required to make your regular mortgage payment—the same as before—and you will become entitled to a tax refund simply by virtue of investing through a cash dam. The act of re-advancing and re-borrowing your mortgage before investing the proceeds in income-generating investments ensures that the interest payments on your ILOC are valid tax deductions.

When you receive your tax refund, you should use it to make a prepayment on your amortizing bad-debt mortgage component. This isn't a hard and fast rule. You are certainly free to spend your tax benefits, generated by your cash dam, in any way you see fit. However, the concept behind cash damming dictates that you should reinvest your tax benefits after you cash dam the proceeds.

Using your tax refund as an extra prepayment on your mortgage has a similar effect as moving to a weekly or a bi-weekly accelerated mortgage schedule from a standard monthly one. As a homeowner, you probably already know that moving to a bi-weekly from a monthly payment schedule will pay off your mortgage faster by virtue of an extra payment or two coming in every year. So when you learn that you can pay down your mortgage by another few hundred dollars each year (using your cash-dam tax refund), it will become apparent that this will compound the effect, knocking another few years off your mortgage.

Basic Leverage Investment Strategy

When it comes to investing, you have a variety of choices depending on what kind of investor you wish to be. However, many investment options have a minimum threshold of entry (e.g. tens of thousands of dollars or more) and won't be available to you at this stage of your financial life. In this stage, you will be limited to investments that can cost effectively be made through a recurring monthly contribution that might be only a few hundred dollars at a time. In all likelihood, this will restrict you to some form of investing in the public markets. After all, you can hardly make a down payment on your first investment property in $500 monthly increments.

The Power of Compound Interest

> "Compound interest is the eighth wonder of the world. He who understands it, earns it...he who doesn't...pays it." — Albert Einstein

When it comes to investing, compounding works in your favour because you earn interest on your original capital as well as on the interest earned. Since the public markets generally rise over the long term, the more time you're able to invest on a recurring monthly basis, the wealthier you will become.

In the book *Lifecycle Investing*, it is argued that time diversification is more important than other types of diversification. Swings between years in the equity markets are actually more volatile than swings between asset classes. History has proven that ten years of investing isn't enough time to be properly time diversified, as markets can fail to go up in a ten-year period. Markets have never failed to improve over any thirty-year period. The evidence from the Yale study described in *Lifecycle Investing* proves that if you start investing twenty years earlier (while you still have a mortgage and must borrow to invest) and give yourself thirty full years to invest in the market in a recurring fashion, the power of compound returns will see your early investments soar in the final decade.

Investor Anxiety

One of the biggest single issues facing a "lump sum" investor is the anxiety that goes along with trying to time the market before taking the big plunge. Few things are more heart-wrenching than making a choice to enter the markets with a substantial investment (e.g. $100,000 or more) and then watching it plummet with a falling market in the following days and months. The single biggest benefit of starting early with small recurring monthly contributions to an investment plan is that it takes out all of the anxiety normally associated with the investment process. For example, if you had invested $100,000 in the market through a regular $833 monthly contribution over the previous ten years, you would have no concerns about any large swings in the TSX. However, if you had held off to make that same $100,000 investment, but as a lump sum in a single transaction, how productive do you think you would be on the following day, especially if you were watching the stock ticker bleed red as the markets took your hard-earned cash with it?

Timing the markets is a fool's game. The most seasoned financial professionals claim no ability to do this, so it would be naive for you to think that you, as an amateur retail investor, would have any better chance of getting it right. One way to ease investor anxiety is to enter the market over a longer period with smaller periodic investments and use dollar-cost averaging to resolve the market timing issue.

Dollar-Cost Averaging (DCA)

Investing $100,000 over ten years in fixed monthly contributions as opposed to waiting to enter the market in a single day has another distinct advantage: dollar-cost averaging (DCA). Many financial experts and media sources tend to confuse DCA with recurring contributions to a retirement fund and may use these terms and strategies interchangeably.

DCA provides an incremental benefit based on a fixed monthly dollar investment. When markets are down, the price per investment unit is lower and your fixed contribution will buy more investment units. Conversely, when markets are up and the price per unit is higher, your fixed monthly investment will purchase fewer units. DCA works because you're effectively timing the market with great precision. It means that you will, relative to the average monthly unit purchase, buy (i.e. buy more) when markets are down and sell (i.e. buy less) when markets are up.

Critics of DCA will argue that there are a few scenarios where it may not work favourably. This may be true; however, no one can argue the benefits of making regular automatic investment contributions over thirty years as opposed to large lump-sum investments when it comes to sleeping well at night!

Borrowing Costs Raise the Floor

It's easy to calculate the return on your investments made from savings or direct contributions from your salary. If you have no debt, you will be investing your own cash, and the return is exactly as published by the investment. If you do have debt (including your mortgage debt), it's appropriate to consider the return on any investment you make to be net of the highest interest that you are paying on your debts. Taking this view will make you think twice about carrying any high-interest credit card debt.

For example, if your $100,000 investment has an annual compound rate of return of 7%, but you're carrying a $100,000 mortgage paying interest at 4%, then your effective net rate of return when you consider the cost of borrowing offset is only 3%. If you carry any high-interest debt balances, you will quickly see any returns on your investments wiped out. The good news is that if you arrange your personal balance sheet properly to line up your debts (including mortgage debt) with your investments, you can lower the effective cost of borrowing by making the debt tax-deductible.

The Break-Even Analysis

The only real difference between investing your own money and investing money that you pulled out of your home is the return on the investments required to break even. When you invest your own money, your break-even point is clearly zero. Any money that you make from your own savings will be providing you a positive return on your investment, assuming that you also get your original investment capital back at the end. When you take out a mortgage on your home to use the money to invest, the difference is that there is now a cost associated with borrowing the money. This cost is equal to the monthly interest you pay the mortgage lender. The variable cost of borrowing money in Canada tends to float around prime lending rates. At the beginning of 2011, prime lending rates hovered around 3%. Therefore, one might assume that the break-even return for any investment made with money borrowed at the prime lending rate would also be 3%, given that this is the actual cost of borrowing the funds in the first place. This is often the case, but you need to consider the tax implications of borrowing and investing to determine the true break-even point.

As an example, when you have an interest-only HELOC at prime (3%) and an investment that is paying you 3% annual interest on a monthly basis, then you will be breaking even, both from a cash flow and from a total return perspective. However, if your investment was providing the same 3% annual return, but this return included dividends, capital gains, or a return of capital, all of which are all more tax efficient than interest income, you're no longer breaking even—you will be making a profit.

To properly understand your break-even point when borrowing to invest, you should first calculate your after-tax cost of borrowing and then calculate your after-tax return on investment. For example, if you're in a 40% tax bracket at the margin and your cost of borrowing money to invest is 3%, then you would calculate your after-tax cost of borrowing by multiplying your cost of borrowing by (1 minus your marginal tax rate): $3\% \times (1 - 40\%) = 1.8\%$. Your actual after-tax borrowing cost on a 3% loan is only 1.8% because the other 1.2% will come back to you as a tax benefit, most likely as a tax refund at the end of the year.

To further illustrate this point, suppose you take out a $200,000 HELOC at 3% to invest it for your retirement. Your interest payments will be exactly $500 per month, and at the end of the year, you will have made $6,000 in interest payments and would have a tax deduction in the same amount. This $6,000 tax deduction will net you a tidy $2,400 tax refund. Therefore, your after-tax cost of borrowing is actually only $3,600 (being the $6,000 interest that you paid less the $2,400 you received as a tax refund). The $3,600 net interest on a $200,000 loan is equal to a 1.8% after-tax cost of borrowing as described above.

On the other side of the equation, when you calculate the return you will make on your investment, you must also adjust for any taxes that might be payable on the income. In our example, if your investment income is in the form of interest only, you will need the full 3% to break even because interest is taxed at 100% of your marginal tax rate. However, if your investment income took some other form that is taxable at a lower rate, such as capital gains, which are taxed at 50% of your marginal tax rate, you would make a $1,200 profit. Even though the cash flows are identical, the tax deduction produced a $2,400 refund, but the taxes payable are only $1,200.

When Does Borrowing to Invest Make Sense?

Borrowing from your home makes sense in circumstances

where your after-tax return on investment exceeds your after-tax cost of borrowing. This is only true, of course, when your risk of losing the original investment is zero. The spread between the return and the cost of borrowing can be very small, and a responsible leverage strategy will still be worthwhile as long as there is no risk of losing your original capital.

For example, you might borrow $200,000 at prime on your home and lend it to a close friend as a first mortgage on their $400,000 home at an interest rate of prime plus 2%. Since you borrowed the money at prime and are collecting interest at prime plus 2%, your net profit is 2%. Of course, in this example, even though there is technically zero risk of loss, as your $200,000 investment is fully secured by your friend's $400,000 property, you might want to consider how you might feel about foreclosing and throwing them out on the street if that becomes the only way to get your original investment back. Maybe that risk isn't worth a 2% return on your money and perhaps you should consider other options with a greater potential return and less emotional stress.

Borrowing to invest can also make sense when your expected return is much greater than your after-tax cost of borrowing and there is some measurable risk of losing a portion of your investment that you're prepared to accept. An example of this kind of investment would be a financial instrument whose value is subject to the public markets. Many mutual funds, or even ETFs, have annualized monthly cash distributions as high as 8% (specific funds change from time to time and are listed at www.mortgagefreedom.ca).

Generally, if an investment related to the public markets is paying a monthly fixed cash distribution at the annualized rate of 8%, it may be substantially composed of dividends and capital gains and typically topped up to the 8% through a return of capital. These types of investments are popular because they are both cash flow positive to leveraged investors and tax efficient at year-end. In this example, your $200,000 loan might still only be costing you 1.8% after tax, but your corresponding $200,000 investment is delivering $1,333.33 each month (i.e. $16,000 per year) in tax-efficient income. One risk with this leveraged investment option is that the value of your original $200,000 investment will fluctuate with the public markets. If you have a long time horizon of at least ten years, this simple investment strategy may be the way to responsibly access the equity in your home and double the size of your nest egg over a twelve- or fifteen-year period without using your own cash savings.

The key to responsible leverage is that you should always undertake it within the context of a plan and with a view to achieving long-term financial goals. You should have a specific financial target or goal and a clear understanding and acceptance of the risks involved.

Who Makes the Rules?

Canadian tax planners and mortgage professionals have been applying the strategy of converting non-deductible debt to deductible debt effectively for three decades. In the beginning, the CRA (formerly Revenue Canada) had its rules. Since then, some versions of the strategy have come before the courts, including the Supreme Court of Canada, and the judges have deliberated on making a few new rules of their own.

We now have the advantage of hindsight. We can examine the recent cases and review the new rules to determine if the methods and techniques described in this book truly meet the test of the income tax legislation in this country and, specifically, the CRA's general anti-avoidance rules (GAAR).

Several pivotal court cases first established and then enshrined the key precedent in Canadian law that paved the way for individual taxpayers to build greater wealth by making their mortgages tax-deductible. The Canadian story actually begins with an English case in 1935 where the Duke of Westminster beat the taxman by winning a landmark decision from the House of Lords, England's highest civil court of the period. It first established the basic principle that we are entitled to arrange our affairs to reduce our tax liability.

This key principle was tested and upheld once again by Vancouver lawyer John Singleton in the Supreme Court of Canada in 2001. The "Singleton Shuffle," or the "debt swap strategy," was reaffirmed to be an acceptable tax-planning strategy in Canada. Once again, a high court upheld the people's fundamental right to arrange their affairs to reduce the tax they owe. Even though Singleton clearly executed the specific financial transactions to avoid taxes, the Supreme Court of Canada concluded that this is acceptable behaviour by a taxpayer.

In the case of the Lipsons versus Canada in 2009, the

Supreme Court of Canada again reassured Canadians that transactions specifically undertaken to make your debt tax-deductible were unimpeachable. These three key court cases, among others, have paved the way for every Canadian taxpayer to actively manage their personal balance sheets with a specific eye to effective tax planning.

Taxpayer's rights are now defined by law and the CRA has now provided an interpretation bulletin[2] to assist borrowers in understanding interest deductibility for properly executing financial plans. This has motivated millions of Canadians to plan their finances more tax efficiently and spawned key strategies such as the Tax Deductible Mortgage Plan (TDMP) to assist them in achieving their long-term financial goals. These court cases are discussed in the Appendix.

Taxpayer Bill of Rights

The Taxpayer Bill of Rights is available on the CRA website for your viewing. If you google it, you will see that there are fifteen taxpayer rights listed, and the first is that "you have the right to receive entitlements and to pay no more and no less than what is required by law." The CRA website goes on to explain that this means "you can expect to receive benefits, credits, and refunds to which you are entitled under the law and to pay no more and no less than the correct amount required under the law." The problem for most Canadians is that calculating "the correct amount required under the law" can be a somewhat intimidating task given the sheer volume and complexity of the tax rules. In any event, your right to effective tax planning is assured under the Canadian Taxpayer Bill of Rights. If you consider building a secure financial future for your family to be a higher priority than paying extraneous taxes, then you need to take a long-term strategic approach to debt management. First and foremost, you should be aware of exercising your first right as a taxpayer and understand the value in aligning your debt against your assets with an eye to tax efficiency.

Cash Damming Financial Benefits

Setting up your cash-damming mortgage strategy will generate modest financial benefits over the first few years, which will improve each year and may amount to several hundred thousand dollars over two or three decades. Restructuring your mortgage for debt conversion and reinvestment of the principal on your regular mortgage payment will contribute a few hundred dollars in tax refunds in the first year, which will grow steadily year over year. The typical first-year tax refund for a routine cash dam will be in the range of $100 to $500.

After a few years of cash damming on your journey to mortgage freedom, you will have built up a substantial nest egg through the regular monthly investment of your mortgage principal payments as you borrow them back. When this nest egg reaches a critical mass, you will be ready to apply an accelerator and advance to the next stage of your journey. In Stage III, you will engage the Tax Deductible Mortgage Plan (TDMP), which accelerates your debt conversion and wealth-building efforts to a whole new level. You will learn how to boost your annual tax benefits tenfold, from a few hundred dollars to a few thousand.

This is where your journey to mortgage freedom starts to get more interesting.

STAGE III
Hit the Gas!
(Accelerate Your Plan)

Welcome to the next level! In Stage III, you will learn about the Tax Deductible Mortgage Plan (TDMP). This is the most exciting phase of your journey to mortgage freedom because you're about to crush all that bad debt on your personal balance sheet, including your mortgage, and move it over in support of your retirement fund. This will achieve two objectives without increasing your debt. First, your debt will all be tax-deductible. Second, you will have the foundation in place to rapidly build wealth for retirement.

In the first two stages, you applied the principles of leverage to first purchase a home and then set up a cash dam by borrowing back your mortgage principal each month and investing it. At this stage, we are going to continue the application of these principles but with a new financial priority. Our new goal is to generate a million dollars or more towards your personal retirement fund without using any of your own money. To do this, we will need to invoke some other source of cash flow and use the prepayment privileges on your mortgage to make significant extra payments of principal on your non-deductible debt every month. These payments will be borrowed back in your deductible line of credit and invested. This form of responsible leverage is a beautiful thing when properly implemented, as it achieves your primary goal of wealth building for retirement through exposure to the markets over a longer period and makes your mortgage tax-deductible. In this section, we will explore the risks and benefits of this advanced leverage investment strategy and the importance of following a plan.

The Tax Deductible Mortgage Plan (TDMP)

The Tax Deductible Mortgage Plan (TDMP) is a fully automated turnkey solution for homeowners who seek professional help in executing this financial and tax strategy. While the mechanics and techniques described in this section may seem complex, it's important to realize that under the TDMP, all these processes will happen automatically on a proprietary technology platform.

By now, you may be thinking that your bad mortgage debt is some kind of evil creature. Your mortgage payment is consuming a huge percentage of your monthly net income and it's the biggest obstacle in the way of your ability to save for retirement. The TDMP allows you to restructure both your mortgage and investments in such a way that converts all your bad mortgage debt into a tax-deductible investment loan in an accelerated manner.

This section of the book will describe what the TDMP is and how it works. There will also be examples of the typical financial benefits you can expect to generate and the risks you must be willing to take to achieve them on your journey to mortgage freedom.

The underlying process of cash damming as described in the previous section continues to support debt conversion, but the main difference is that the TDMP rapidly accelerates the process and ultimately generates much greater wealth for retirement. This advanced debt conversion strategy introduces new transactions on a monthly basis and requires a rigid and precise schedule of money movements, all of which are automated in the TDMP. Homeowners who attempt to execute a similar process on a manual basis with their bank often feel frustrated at the level of effort required to keep the debt conversion process going. A professionally managed service like that offered at TDMP.com removes these administrative hurdles.

TDMP-managed services are described in a series of videos at www.tdmp.com. As a homeowner, you can also take the TDMP Test on the website to determine if you qualify and to review the financial benefits it might offer you. When you engage this strategy through an independent TDMP Certified Mortgage Planner, all the services described herein will be performed on your behalf, so you don't really need to understand the detailed mechanics of what might be going on each week during the monthly cycle. However, as stated earlier, it's important to understand the target benefits and the risks involved and, as with any advanced mortgage strategy, to ensure you're comfortable with the risk profile before you engage the plan. This is the primary focus of this section of the book.

Why the TDMP?

At this stage, your overriding financial priority is to convert all of your bad mortgage debt into a good (i.e. tax-deductible) investment loan as quickly as possible. You will achieve this by reconfiguring your existing leveraged investments or using your home equity to acquire a new special-purpose investment that will generate the right amount of tax-efficient cash flow required to convert your mortgage on a prescribed accelerated schedule.

The TDMP debt conversion allows you to defer significant taxes and deduct investment loan interest and use this money to make additional prepayments against the principal portion of your mortgage each year. As in the previous stage, all homeowners are unilaterally advised to apply the incremental tax benefits generated by their mortgage strategy back into the plan by making prepayments against the principal on their mortgage. This will result in paying off non-deductible mortgage debt many years ahead of the original schedule, typically in one third of the regular amortization period.

Do You Qualify?

Mortgage qualification criteria and investment compliance guidelines ensure that only those who are suitable and well qualified engage in the TDMP. The following basic guidelines determine suitability:

1. The TDMP is for highly qualified homeowners only.
2. A minimum of 30% equity in the home is recommended.
3. The homeowner should have non-deductible debt, including their mortgage, equal to at least 20% of the value of the home.
4. You need a minimum credit score of approximately 680 with a clean credit history that shows no delinquency or anomalous borrowing patterns.
5. Your total debt-servicing cost should not exceed 40% of your income.
6. You should have at least ten years before you plan to retire.
7. At least one regulator requires that you be under sixty years old.

Most TDMP homeowners are in their thirties, forties, or their early fifties with high incomes and excellent credit scores. You may be older or younger than that, which still might be okay, as long as you can otherwise qualify for the home equity line of credit (HELOC) as well as the TDMP Accelerator described below.

If you require debt consolidation advice or believe that you have less than perfect credit, you should consult your independent mortgage professional to determine which path to take. You may still be able to refinance for debt consolidation purposes or even get a HELOC and enter Stage II of your journey to mortgage freedom.

This strategy is for sophisticated and well-qualified homeowners who have made a plan to transfer their leverage from their home to their retirement fund. While the recommended minimum home equity requirement is 30%, the more equity you have available in your home, the greater the wealth benefits will be. You need to be able to prove that you earn enough income to be eligible to refinance into a HELOC. Your mortgage professional can advise on exactly what that means if you aren't sure.

The TDMP Accelerator

The main difference between Stage II and Stage III is the introduction of a TDMP Accelerator. To optimize your debt conversion from bad debt to good debt and to maximize your tax benefits, you must accelerate your cash-damming schedule. The TDMP Accelerator is another powerful tool in your journey to mortgage freedom. It's a special-purpose investment vehicle with the primary objective of generating the monthly tax-efficient cash flow required to make an extra payment against your mortgage every month until you eliminate all your bad debt. Ideally, these additional payments along with the reinvestment of your tax benefits will allow you to pay out your mortgage completely in approximately one third of the natural amortizing period. For example, if a mortgage is amortizing over twenty-five years, the cash flow from the TDMP Accelerator will demolish the mortgage in less than eight years through additional monthly prepayments of principal.

Capital preservation is a secondary objective since you will finance the TDMP Accelerator from borrowed money. Some day you may ultimately choose to liquidate the TDMP Accelerator and pay out the loan you used to acquire it. This liquidation will typically occur at some point after you reduce your bad mortgage debt to zero, as described in Stage IV. Several forms of TDMP Accelerator investments can satisfy these objectives, including mutual funds, exchange-traded funds, investment properties, or cash flows from your own business venture.

Keep in mind that the objectives of the TDMP Accelerator investments are quite different than those in Stage II. The TDMP is primarily concerned with monthly cash flow. At this new stage of your journey to mortgage freedom, your primary financial goal has switched to crushing your mortgage, and this will require predictable, tax- efficient, monthly cash flow. As such, you will select different investments in consultation with your financial advisor.

Why It Works

The concept is quite simple. As an example, let's assume that in the previous stage, you were able to build up a leverage investment portfolio of $150,000 by cash damming your mortgage. In all likelihood, you have taken no income or other cash distributions from this portfolio, as you reinvested any income generated along the way. Alternatively, if you're just starting your journey to mortgage freedom now and have enough equity in your home to start the TDMP immediately (without the prior experience of cash damming), we assume that you have the ability to access $150,000 either directly on your new HELOC or as a combination of HELOC and investment loans.

In either case, in this stage you will use this $150,000

to acquire the cash-generating assets that will constitute your TDMP Accelerator, sometimes referred to as a TDMP Cash Flow Portfolio. The key here is that the entire portfolio must consist of assets that distribute predictable monthly cash distributions.

TDMP Assumptions

Let's assume that your $150,000 TDMP Accelerator is invested in assets that provide you with an 8% annual cash flow. This equates to $1,000 each month, which you're going to use to make an extra monthly payment on your mortgage. However, the 8% annual cash flow is rather arbitrary, so feel free to use a more conservative cash distribution if that more accurately reflects the projected cash distributions of the investments you have chosen for your own personal TDMP Accelerator.

Any predictable cash flow distribution between 6% and 8% will work for the TDMP and still be cash flow positive when borrowing costs are less than 6%. At the time of publication, borrowing costs float in the range of 3% and 4%, so there are no cash flow issues in creating a TDMP Accelerator that only generates 6%. However, there are also many assets available, including a number of mutual funds from just about every large fund company, that continue to provide cash distributions in the order of 8%.

It's important, however, not to confuse the cash distribution of an investment with its actual return. The cash distribution and the rate of return are two different things. Cash distribution is the income that the asset is set to deliver on a monthly basis and it's generally a combination of dividends and capital gains. If the monthly distribution of a mutual fund is fixed at 8%, it will be topped up by return of capital in any year where the actual return on the investment falls below 8%. The concept of investments that provide predictable (fixed) cash distributions was originally conceived to smooth out the income provided to investors while still providing the opportunity for greater actual returns through exposure to volatile equities.

The historical real return on equities throughout 138 years of history from 1871 until 2009 was 7.87% even after the market fall in 2008. This is why—in addition to 8% cash-distributing mutual funds being commonplace—we will use 8% as both the rate of return as well as the cash distribution in our example.

The final assumption that we will use is a cost of borrowing equal to 5.30% for the amortizing mortgage to reflect today's posted mortgage rates and 5.75% for the revolving investment line of credit. Both of these rates are approximately 2% higher than the best available mortgage rates at the time of writing in January 2011, so the use of higher interest rates in the example is quite conservative.

TDMP Schedule

The primary action of the TDMP is to boost your retirement fund by moving the debt you have on your home over to your retirement fund. Applying the principle of leverage at a young age has been proven to build you greater wealth for retirement at less risk. In Canada, it must be understood that a key benefit of transferring the leverage in your home over to your retirement fund is the conversion of bad mortgage debt into good (tax-deductible) mortgage debt. This is because the mortgage on your home isn't tax-deductible, but the mortgage on your retirement fund is. The point of the plan is to achieve this transfer as fast as possible on an accelerated schedule, which is another reason why you should select investments that generate a higher cash distribution.

The key consideration that sets the TDMP apart from simple cash damming, as described in the previous section, is that the substantial interest payment on the HELOC debt must be serviced on time every month and the cash must be available in the bank account to make that happen. Assuming a 5.75% cost of borrowing on the $150,000 HELOC investment loan, the TDMP process requires that you make a $718.75 interest payment on the same day every month. The TDMP monthly cash flow schedule is a rigorous monthly cycle of money movements that is driven primarily by the requirement to make this interest payment and to ensure, through the process, that this monthly $718.75 will qualify as a tax deduction under CRA rules. This requirement drives the schedule described in detail below.

TDMP Case Study Assumptions

To visualize the monthly TDMP cash flows, we will look at a hypothetical case study of a fully accelerated TDMP where mutual funds are being used as the TDMP Accelerator. The case study results are based on the following assumptions:

- You have a property with an appraised value of $500,000.

- Your starting mortgage balance is $250,000 amortized over twenty-five years and includes a consolidation of all outstanding non-deductible debt, including credit cards and other high-interest loans.
- A monthly mortgage payment is $1,500 (starting principal portion of $400).
- An average mortgage interest rate of 5.30%
- An average line-of-credit interest rate of 5.75%.
- A monthly cash deposit from the TDMP Accelerator based on an 8% annual distribution.
- An investment growth rate of 8%.
- A marginal tax rate of 39%.

TDMP Setup

If you aren't already in a fully functioning Stage II cash dam, the first step is to refinance your mortgage and replace it with a new, multi-component, re-advanceable home equity line of credit (HELOC) as described in Stage II of this book. It's vital that the HELOC have the capability of being re-advanced back to the original balance any time there is a principal payment applied to the amortizing mortgage component. Not all bank HELOC products are created equal. Some don't allow multiple components and others don't have the capability to re-advance automatically. Your TDMP Certified Mortgage Planner will be able to advise what HELOCs are suitable for the TDMP.

Financing the HELOC at 80% of the appraised value of the home brings the total loan value to $400,000 in our example. However, paying out all of the existing bad debt will require only $250,000; therefore, $150,000 is now available as the starting balance in our revolving component of the new HELOC, or investment line of credit (ILOC). The $150,000 will be drawn down to finance the purchase of the TDMP Accelerator. For the purposes of the case study, the investments consist of mutual funds that provide predictable monthly cash distributions at 8% and are assumed to provide a long-term actual return at this same rate.

The second step in the setup process is to open up a new bank account. This account must be a dedicated no-fee chequing account that can both accept deposits and make pre-authorized payments. It should also provide you with cheques so you can accommodate off-schedule investment purchases required occasionally to clear out surplus balances that accumulate over time. We'll call this account a tax-clearing bank account (TCBA) in the TDMP process. The TCBA will then be "connected" to your ILOC so you can make interest payments. The interest payments are tax-deductible and the TCBA statements will serve as an audit trail for CRA purposes should the need ever arise to prove your entitlement to these deductions. Your regular household chequing account will be connected to the $250,000 amortizing mortgage debt, where you will make regular monthly mortgage payments as before. Once setup is complete, you will make your regular mortgage payments and the rest will be automated.

TDMP Monthly Cash Flow Cycle

Once the monthly cash flow cycle has been setup, your cash flows will look like this:

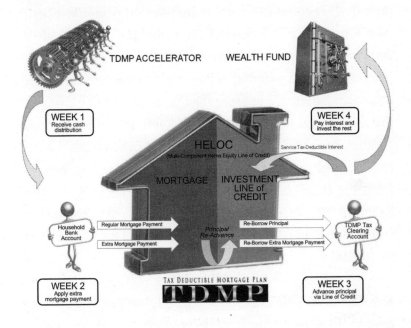

The TDMP monthly cash flow cycle is very predictable. Once you have opened and properly configured the accounts for the recurring movement of money, the cash flow cycle can be broken down into four weekly sets of transactions as follows:

Week 1 – The TDMP Accelerator annual cash distribution is fixed at 8% ($12,000 each year), which amounts to twelve equal monthly payments of $1,000. This $1,000 arrives in your regular bank account during the first week of each and every month.

Week 2 – An extra mortgage payment will be automatically applied to the principal balance of your $250,000 amortizing mortgage (your bad debt). This extra payment (100% principal) is equal to the cash distribution from the TDMP Accelerator (i.e. $1,000). This principal payment is in addition to the principal portion of your regular mortgage payments, which you will make on a monthly or accelerated schedule, the same as before. The principal portion from the regular mortgage payment (e.g. $400 in month one) in addition to the $1,000 extra payment will be automatically re-advanced and immediately available for you to borrow from the ILOC component of your new HELOC. In this example, the total amount of principal paid down on the amortizing loan is $1,400; therefore, the ILOC will increase by $1,400.

Week 3 – You will draw down the $1,400 newly available in your ILOC and deposit it into your new tax-clearing bank account (TCBA). It's critical to get the money into the TCBA on time each month because the interest payment due on the money borrowed to purchase the $150,000 TDMP Accelerator is scheduled to come out on the 26th of each month. These interest payments are tax-deductible and will be paid out of the TCBA along with any tax-deductible carrying charges that apply. In this example, payments are conservatively estimated at approximately $800.

Week 4 – Any balance remaining in the TCBA (approximately $600) must be invested. This is another CRA rule required to ensure the deductibility of all interest on the right side of the diagram. Your financial advisor will make this investment automatically, using a pre-authorized contribution, in accordance with your prior instructions.

Benefits

The assumptions set out in this case study will generate the following benefits:

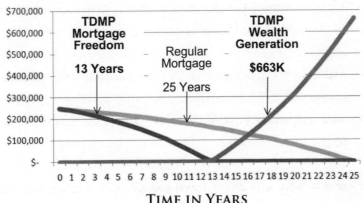

TIME IN YEARS

- A first-year tax benefit from the TDMP (tax refund) of $3,364. This is estimated by multiplying the monthly interest payment by 12 and then by your marginal tax rate, which is assumed to be 39%. TDMP cash flows are predictable within the plan, and as long as interest rates remain fairly stable during the year, your tax benefits can be quite accurately predicted. Note that this benefit will be offset by any income tax payable due to the TDMP Accelerator cash distributions. The taxable nature of various forms of income is discussed later in this section.

- TDMP mortgage freedom occurs in the thirteenth year as opposed to the normal twenty-five year amortization period. In year thirteen, the TDMP wealth fund will have grown to a point where it equals the outstanding balance on the investment line of credit and you could choose to be mortgage-free by selling investments to retire debt. Note that there may be tax liabilities triggered when you sell investments. A TDMP-approved tax accountant should be consulted prior to liquidation of the portfolios for any reason.

- Future savings (equal to twelve years' mortgage payments) of $216,000. This is the amount of savings you will achieve by paying off your bad-debt amortizing mortgage twelve years faster than the original amortization period. However, this benefit doesn't factor in any inflation or investment growth.

- A net twenty-five-year incremental wealth benefit of $663,000. This is the key number and primary goal of the strategy. Your net incremental growth of your retirement fund is calculated net of the ILOC balance and equal to $663,000! You are almost $700,000 richer by applying the principles of responsible leverage to building your nest egg by transferring your home leverage over to your retirement fund!

Another fundamental feature of the TDMP strategy and a key differentiating feature when compared to other investment strategies is that all of the TDMP financial benefits are achieved without requiring any cash from your own pocket. Where most financial strategies require an out-of-pocket contribution to purchase the initial investments or pay down debt, the TDMP doesn't. This strategy uses your existing home mortgage for the leverage and an internal cash flow system that ensures the entire process is self-funding.

The most notable short-term financial benefit is the first annualized (or full year) TDMP tax benefit of $3,364. All tax benefits are reinvested in the strategy after first being applied as extra mortgage payments on your amortizing loan (bad debt).

The TDMP process is complete on the day you finally pay off your amortizing (bad debt) mortgage. The most important change after you pay off your amortizing mortgage is that the cash you had earmarked for your regular monthly mortgage payments is no longer required for that purpose and you can reallocate it directly into future investments or to the reduction of tax-deductible debt. If you decide to invest it, the result will be the generation of close to $700,000 in incremental wealth at the end of twenty-five years based on the assumptions set out in the case study and as compared to your neighbours who simply pay off their mortgage over the full twenty-five-year term and have no investments or tax deductions.

Risk

Risk is a key subject in this section. Sometimes the word itself strikes fear into the heart of the ordinary homeowner and novice investor because they confuse it with the word *loss*, which is truly something to be feared. Nobody likes to lose—especially money! Since the natural consequence of risk is failure, loss is possible when you take a risk. Some risks are necessary and cannot be avoided. However, if such a risk can be measured, it can often be mitigated when you think strategically and are following a long-term plan. We will review risk in the context of the mitigating strategies inherent to the TDMP strategy.

To achieve mortgage freedom, you should review and deliberately consider possible risks at each stage of the plan. At the end of this analysis, you will decide what risks are worth the potential financial benefits and what risks aren't. In all likelihood, the greatest risk you will assume on your lifetime journey to mortgage freedom is the extreme leverage that accompanied the original high-ratio mortgage that you required to get on the property ladder in the first place. Assuming you leveraged your original home purchase with a mortgage at a 9:1 or 19:1 ratio, with zero tax efficiency, this will be your highest point of risk. Thereafter, you will reduce your risk exposure as you de-leverage the original debt into the conventional range (e.g. 4:1) and then again as your debt becomes tax-deductible when you transfer this leverage from your home to your retirement fund.

To achieve the financial benefits offered by the TDMP and without having to use any of your own cash, there are three categories of risk to consider as follows:

1. Cash flow risk (the intersection between market risk and interest rate risk)
2. Canada Revenue Agency (CRA) risk
3. Contingency risk (where you might need to withdraw cash from your plan)

Cash flow risk focuses on the spread between the cash coming in from the TDMP Accelerator and the cost of servicing the loans taken to purchase the underlying assets. Cash flow risk is essentially the intersection of market risk and interest rate risk. Market risk is the chance of a sustained down period in the market during the early years of debt conversion. The risk is the possibility of not achieving your target 8% returns (or anything close to it) and that your 8% cash distributions start to erode as a result. Interest rate risk is the possibility of your cost of borrowing skyrocketing.

In the worst-case scenario, the adverse consequences of cash flow risk happen in the event that your cost of borrowing (interest rates) rises at the same time as the market falls. In this circumstance, it's quite possible that you could face a negative cash flow situation and would be required to inject some cash from your own pocket into the TDMP plan until the market corrects itself and spreads return to normal levels. The cash flow management services provided by TDMP.com mitigate this risk and protect you by adjusting transaction amounts within the monthly cash flows to maintain the spread during times of compression. Annual cash flow reviews proactively monitor available and future sources of cash flow to ensure that debt servicing requirements are met before investment contributions are advanced. There are many sources of cash that will be put to work before you are into your own pocket, including the principal payments on your mortgage, your tax refunds, and the funds that have accumulated in your wealth portfolio.

Cash flow risk is a much more material risk in the first few years, because after the fifth year, you will have amassed considerable funds (mainly due to tax refunds) and your wealth portfolio will be substantial enough to fund any cash shortfall. Financial advisors may consider cash flow risk to be remote under stable market conditions with normal spreads between long-term market returns and the cost of borrowing, but the risk is never zero. Since the cost of borrowing on investment loans and lines of credit are based on a fluctuating prime lending rate, constant monitoring and proactive cash flow management is required. It may be interesting to note that in 2008, as the markets suffered their worst decline in history, governments moved quickly to reduce interest rates to reverse the decline and end the recession. The outcome for TDMP customers was that they didn't go cash flow negative at any time during this period. While cash distributions from investments in 2009 may have dropped as much as 50% in some cases, variable interest rates dropped over 60% (from 5.75% to 2.25%) in the same period.

If you believe that Canadian monetary policy will react to future declines in the stock market by reducing interest rates as they did in 2008, then you would have to consider the risk of the TDMP financial strategy going cash flow negative to be remote and therefore acceptable in light of the potential financial upside.

Canada Revenue Agency (CRA) risk has two components: abusive tax avoidance and cash damming.

In 1988, the federal government implemented the general anti-avoidance rule (GAAR), where they declared that a taxpayer who restructures debt or performs some other transaction with the *sole purpose* of gaining a tax benefit is guilty of abusive tax avoidance. In summary, this is only a risk if you attempt to convert your mortgage into good debt without actually investing. The TDMP fully mitigates this risk, and you can provide proof that you used your monies for eligible investments by producing your tax-clearing bank account (TCBA) statements. When you transfer your leverage from your home to your retirement fund, which is the whole point of the TDMP, you have now borrowed to invest and there is no CRA risk.

The CRA has defined and approved cash damming but advises the use of separate bank accounts to avoid the possibility of commingling funds. You can completely mitigate this risk by following the CRA's guidelines on cash damming and by keeping cash flows in separate bank accounts. The biggest risk to you, the homeowner, is in accidentally mixing your personal finances with your investments or tax-deductible finances. The TDMP mitigates this risk through the TCBA. You must use every dollar you advance from your ILOC into your TCBA for one of three purposes:

1. Paying the interest on tax-deductible interest (i.e. ILOC).
2. Paying qualifying carrying charges for a service that manages these cash flows (i.e. the TDMP).
3. Investing the money with the intent to make a profit directly in assets that have the capability of paying income.

As long as you never use funds from the TCBA for personal purposes, the audit trail will remain clean and will constitute an audit history that will satisfy the CRA.

Contingency risk relates to the possibility of an emergency and needing some of the money in your plan. As with any long-term investment strategy, diversification over time is our friend when it comes to growth, but it can present unknowns in other areas. A time may come when a job loss, health emergency, school fees, or other financial strain requires you to access emergency cash. While homeowners aren't allowed to access funds from the TCBA for personal use, you can get money out of the TDMP—you simply must do it in a prescribed manner under CRA rules. We achieve this by essentially hitting the TDMP "pause" button. When you need cash from the plan, you can suspend the monthly investment (i.e. the $600 investment into the wealth fund) and back up cash flows into your regular bank account where you're free to withdraw funds for personal use.

Furthermore, you can retain tax refunds for your personal use if you think you might need the money, and your TDMP wealth fund is always available in an emergency since it's not secured by any debt obligation.

TDMP Managed Services—A Team Approach

Implementing the TDMP is a complex and time-consuming process, and some of the cash flows can be difficult to set up. Furthermore, rigorous monthly administration requires constant monitoring of transactions moving into and out of each of your accounts. Annual tax preparation and filing can also be somewhat complex, while mortgage renewals, midterm refinances, and even moving into new houses in the years to come will create additional documentation requirements in case they are ever requested by the CRA. Homeowners considering the TDMP should seek professional advice to ensure the plan is properly configured and that investment and tax advice is current and compliant with CRA guidelines. TDMP.com provides a fully managed service covering all aspects of the plan from initial consultation and qualification to mortgage funding, investment purchases, monthly administration, and annual tax services. Several advisors typically work together as your TDMP team:

TDMP Certified Mortgage Planner – The process typically starts with the mortgage planner, who will provide an initial qualification assessment, prepare a full TDMP Benefits Report, and take a mortgage application. Mortgage financing into a suitable multi-component re-advanceable home equity line of credit (HELOC) will include a debt review and recommendations for consolidation of any outstanding credit card balances and other debts into the new mortgage structure.

TDMP Approved Financial Advisor – To meet regulatory guidelines and to avoid potential conflicts of interest, your TDMP-approved financial advisor may be separate from your mortgage advisor. This advisor will provide the necessary investment advice in setting up the TDMP Accelerator and wealth fund. You will meet with this advisor on at least an annual basis to review the performance of your investments in context of your long-term financial goals and retirement plans.

TDMP Cash Flow Manager – Your cash flow manager is

your point of contact throughout the life of the plan and will serve to quarterback any requests you have relating to cash flows, investments, taxes, or mortgage payments. This includes liaising with the mortgage lender on your behalf and requesting monthly mortgage prepayments and line-of-credit advances based on your authorizations. Each year, your cash flow manager will conduct a complete review of your TCBA to ensure:

- monthly transactions are processed correctly;
- no additional transactions are flowing through the account that could put the tax-deductible status of the line of credit at risk;
- an adequate minimum balance is maintained in the account to act as a buffer against unexpected transactions or delays in fund movements;
- annual adjustments to monthly mutual fund cash distributions are implemented in time for the February mortgage prepayment (these normally take effect in January); and
- optimal funds are invested on a monthly basis.

TDMP-Approved Tax Accountant – Your tax accountant will play an increasingly important role in your plan as the years go by. In addition to preparing and filing your tax returns, your accountant will also work closely with your cash flow manager, as required, to accurately document any mortgage restructuring due to moving into new houses, refinancing, or any other life event that may affect the structure of your debt.

Each year, your accountant will provide an annual cover letter to the CRA to summarize your TDMP cash-damming strategy and eligible deductions and prepare a statement of investment income for inclusion with your T1 general return. They may also respond to the CRA on your behalf for all matters relating to additional documentation requirements, audits, challenges, or reassessments of your tax returns.

Consider the scenario where the CRA audits you after you have been running this program for seven years. When the auditor comes to visit, you must prove your entitlement to the substantial tax refunds you have received over the years. Remember that you must be prepared to produce a complete history of statements from the TCBA and demonstrate that every dollar processed through that bank account you used for a qualifying purpose under CRA rules. No one looks forward to a CRA audit, but if you do happen to be selected for one, you will be glad to have your records in good order.

Investment Options

In Stage II, when you were investing using a monthly pre-authorized cheque or other regular small monthly investments, your options were limited. If you used an advisor, you would likely have been in mutual funds, and if you were using a self-directed strategy in an online account, you may have made other choices. Mutual funds remain a clear and accessible option, but there are other options as well.

Mutual Funds

Mutual funds are a highly popular investment option for

millions of Canadians. A mutual fund is a professionally managed pool of investments. Their popularity in Canada is driven by their simplicity, which is a great benefit to any homeowner with a limited knowledge of or interest in investments. Even though you may be keenly motivated to achieve your long-term financial targets, the investment advice and product selection along the way is often better left to professionals.

There are five key benefits to mutual funds that make them attractive investments in general and one of the most popular options for cash damming your mortgage:

1. Diversification
2. Cost efficiency
3. Liquidity
4. Cash flow convenience
5. Professional management

Diversification. The first rule of investing is asset diversification. Nothing reduces portfolio risk more than diversifying assets widely across different industry sectors, asset classes, and nations. Mutual funds are the answer for the millions of ordinary investors who simply don't have the large amount of cash available in their individual portfolios to achieve adequate diversification.

Cost efficiency. Economies of scale make mutual funds a cost-effective investment option, especially when the investments consist of small amounts. You share the costs across a large pool of investors, including the costs associated with your individual transactions and the management fees for professional investment advice.

Liquidity. An investor may redeem all or any portion of their mutual fund shares or units on any given business day. Some restrictions may apply, but, generally speaking, mutual funds are liquid at the net asset value per share (NAVPS), which is calculated daily based on the current market value of the underlying individual securities held in the portfolio.

Cash flow convenience. Mutual fund companies provide investors with a convenient and efficient way to meet investment goals by offering pre-authorized chequing plans (PACs), also known as pre-authorized deposit plans (PADs), to be set up in any amount for a recurring monthly contribution to a fund. This is highly convenient when you're cash damming the principal from your monthly mortgage payment and reinvesting it in small increments every month. In addition, automatic or systematic withdrawal plans (AWDs or SWPs) can be set up to deposit the cash distribution from a mutual fund on a recurring basis. Many mutual fund companies also offer attractive features such as automatic reinvestment of fund distributions and free transfers between mutual funds of the same family.

Professional management. Mutual funds are managed by an individual or team of professionally trained and experienced fund managers. These professionals offer you the benefit of skilled advice that you would not otherwise have access to with a small investment portfolio. In addition, since the operating costs are spread across the entire pool of investors in the mutual fund, the cost of this professional advice can be minimized.

Mutual funds are often maligned in the media, and the major disadvantage is usually related to costs. Although they are a cost efficient way of investing small sums of money, they are not necessarily the most cost efficient way of investing a larger sum. However, since their introduction in the early '80s, Canadians have invested over $600 billion in mutual funds. Pooling money in this manner has allowed modest individual portfolios to grow faster due to economies of scale and broader access to professional advice.

Exchange-Traded Funds (ETFs)

ETFs are like mutual funds that trade on the stock market. The first ETF entered the market in 1993 and they have gained popularity among investors because of their low cost, tax efficiency, and the fact that they can be traded like a stock. Most ETFs track an index. The costs are lower because there is less management required to simply track an index.

Professionally managed ETF portfolios are gaining ground in Canada and some claim significant benefits over mutual funds, including lower costs, better returns, and tax benefits. Managed ETF portfolios that provide predictable tax-efficient monthly cash flow to investors and are otherwise well suited to accelerated debt-conversion strategies may be suitable for the TDMP Accelerator.

Self-Employed Business Loans

If you're self-employed and unincorporated, cash damming the revenue from your business is an absolute no-brainer. Whether you own an investment property that you rent out or whether you buy and sell widgets on eBay matters not. What's important here is that you have a source of business revenue and related expenses.

Normally, if you run a business, you will have a dedicated business bank account where you deposit the revenue and from which you pay your business expenses. Let's use the example of a rental property, where you routinely deposit a rent cheque on the first day of the month and thereafter pay out related expenses including the mortgage payment, property taxes, and maintenance fees.

To keep the math simple, let's assume that the investment property mortgage payments are interest only and that the monthly rent is $2,000, which just happens to match the total cost of the monthly expenses. Each month in your business bank account, you can see $2,000 deposited on the first of the month and then the balance systematically drops back to the original level as the expenses come out.

To set up a cash dam, you will make the following adjustment to your monthly cash flow (note: as always, you must be in a multi-component re-advanceable HELOC for this to work):

1. Each month, you deposit the $2,000 rent cheque into your personal bank account instead of your business bank account.
2. You make a prepayment on your mortgage of $2,000.

3. The HELOC re-advances your revolving investment line of credit by $2,000.
4. You instruct your lender to draw down the available $2,000 from the investment line of credit and deposit it in your business bank account.

The effect of this cash dam in this example will be to convert $24,000 of bad-debt mortgage into a $24,000 good-debt (tax-deductible) line of credit loaned to yourself to run your own business each year. Over five years, you will have converted $120,000 of bad debt into good debt and the interest that your business (you) pays on this line of credit is a valid business expense and is therefore tax-deductible.

The Fringe Division

The fringe division is a blanket category for all other potential investments that might be suitable for your portfolio on the journey to mortgage freedom but are unregulated or marginally regulated. While some of these investments may be highly suitable for specific individuals, the fact that they are not regulated in the normal manner or are exempt from the requirement to file a prospectus introduces another form of investor risk best described as "buyer beware."

A mortgage investment corporation (MIC), for example, can be an interesting investment option for those who don't like the volatility of the public markets. MICs generally hold high-interest mortgages and pay dividends to shareholders, which must be treated as interest for tax purposes. It's not difficult to see how an MIC invested in a pool of mortgages that is paying interest at 12% should be able to distribute cash to its shareholders at an attractive rate of 8% or 9%. Although returns can be attractive and volatility is low, these MICs are typically quite small and there is a significant risk that you could lose your money if they are mismanaged or if their mortgages default.

Investment Income and Tax Ramifications

The Importance of Your Marginal Tax Bracket

In Canada, it's important to understand that we have a graduated tax system where the more money you earn, the more taxes you'll pay as a percentage of your income. Your marginal tax rate is the tax rate that will be applied to the last dollar you earned. In the table below, you will see the Ontario marginal tax rates for 2010. If you earn $50,000 per year in taxable income, you will be required to pay the government 31.15 cents on the last dollar you earned because you are in the 31.15% marginal tax bracket. If you make $130,000 per year, you are in Ontario's highest marginal tax bracket and you will pay 46.41% to the government at the margin (i.e. on the last dollar you earned). The combination of your provincial tax rate plus your federal tax rate is equal to your marginal tax rate.

2010 Ontario Marginal Tax Rate (Federal and Provincial)

Taxable Annual Income	Marginal Tax Rate	Capital Gains Tax Rate	Eligible Dividends Tax Rate
$0 - $37,106	20.05%	10.03%	0.00%
$37,107 - $40,970	24.15%	12.08%	0.00%
$40,970 - $65,345	31.15%	15.58%	9.76%
$65,345 - $74,214	32.98%	16.49%	10.55%
$74214 - $76,986	35.59%	17.70%	14.02%
$76,986 - $81,941	39.41%	19.70%	16.49%
$81,941 - $127,021	43.41%	21.70%	22.25%
$127,021 and over	46.41%	23.20%	26.57%

Your average tax rate is different from your marginal tax rate. Your average tax rate is equal to the total income tax you pay divided by your taxable income. Therefore, your average tax rate will always be lower than your marginal tax rate. Ernst & Young have an excellent tax calculator on their website at http://www.ey.com/CA/en/Services/Tax/Tax-Calculators-2010-Personal-Tax if you wish to calculate your marginal and average tax rates in any province. You can use this calculator to see that while $50,000 in taxable income puts you in the 31.15% marginal tax bracket, your average tax rate is only 18.35%, as you will pay $9,177 in income tax.

When you hear high-income earners complain about paying half their income to the government in income taxes, the fact is that there is no higher tax bracket than 46.41% in Ontario, and although the provincial tax rates vary by province, there is no income tax bracket higher than 50% in this country. As your income increases above $127,000, your average tax rate will be closer to your marginal tax rate. For example, if your taxable income is $130,000, you will pay $40,767 income tax if you live in Ontario, which means that your average tax rate is only 31.36% even though you are in the highest marginal tax rate at 46.41%. But if your 2010 taxable income was $2 million, the Ernst & Young calculator shows that your average tax rate is 45.53%, which is much closer to the marginal rate of 46.41%. Of course, if your taxable income is in the $2 million range, you have to seriously question yourself as to why you would bother reading this book.

Interest, Dividends, and Capital Gains

When considering financial strategies and the holdings in your portfolio, it's important to be mindful of the income tax rates when deciding what type of assets you should hold in your registered plans (e.g. your RRSP) versus what you should hold in your non-registered (e.g. the TDMP) portfolios. In the table above, you can see that the marginal tax rate is much higher than either the capital gains tax rate or the Canadian eligible dividend tax rate. In fact, the capital gains tax rate is equal to exactly 50% of your marginal tax rate and the tax rate for dividend income is also significantly lower than your marginal tax rate. All other types of investment income, including interest income, will be taxed at your highest (marginal) tax rate.

Fixed-income assets, such as bonds and mortgages, generate interest income that will be taxed at the current marginal tax rate if they are held in non-registered accounts. Therefore, it generally makes good sense to hold this class of investments in your registered accounts, where they are sheltered from taxation: in an RRSP or in a TFSA.

On the other hand, you can see from the above table that you pay no tax on eligible dividend income if your other taxable income is under $37,106 and much lower tax than your marginal tax rate in every bracket. Therefore, the better place to hold stocks, equity mutual funds, and equity ETFs is in your non-registered accounts. If the only place you were to hold dividend-paying assets were in your RRSP, you would effectively forfeit the benefit of the dividend tax credit. Furthermore, capital losses can, in a non-registered account, decrease your net taxes in the year that the losses are realized. In your RRSP, however, capital losses are just losses.

As you will read in the final stage of your journey to mortgage freedom (Stage IV), if you wish to keep your leveraged TDMP portfolio of dividend-paying investments into retirement, you should seriously consider the option of becoming debt-free without selling assets by moving your HELOC into your own RRSP. If your RRSP is already structured to hold your fixed-income investments, including bonds and mortgages, where interest income grows on a tax-sheltered basis, you will be in an excellent position to consider this home stretch option. As you prepare to stop working, you should also be planning your retirement financial strategy mindful of the likelihood that your taxable income may fall into a lower marginal tax bracket.

Interest Deductibility with Return of Capital

You can implement TDMP Accelerators with a variety of underlying assets, each with their own risks and benefits.

Your financial advisor will help you select the ones most suitable for you. The one common feature is the ability to produce a predictable monthly cash flow that you can use to make an extra payment every month against the principal balance of your mortgage, thereby crushing your mortgage debt on a vastly accelerated schedule.

A popular option for many Canadians is to finance their TDMP Accelerator by borrowing from home equity and purchasing market investments specifically designed to make regular cash distributions, usually monthly. The purpose of this section is not to extol the benefits of any one over the other, but to raise awareness of a common feature used by these types of trusts and funds: return of capital (ROC). ROC refers to a payment made to the investor of all or a portion of the original investment and should not be confused with return *on* capital, which represents the rate of return of the investment.

ROC is popular with certain market investments because it lets investors know what their cash flow will be regardless of short-term market fluctuations. As a result, and because of the tax efficiencies inherent to the distribution, they are ideal for the TDMP, allowing you to turn the entire monthly distribution into an extra payment against your mortgage. However, ROC distributions come with their own rules and complexities that you must both understand and abide by at tax time.

Let's look at an example. Assume you borrow $100,000 from your line of credit to finance the purchase of a TDMP Accelerator comprised of a mutual fund that will distribute 6% annually and make the distributions on a monthly basis.

This means that each month, $500 will be deposited into your personal bank account. For the purpose of this example, let's assume the entire amount will be attributed to ROC. Since you borrowed the money to purchase the mutual fund in the first place, you will have an interest payment to make on your line of credit. Based on a 4% borrowing rate and interest-only payment, you will need $334 each month to service the loan. Since the entire $100,000 was used to purchase a qualifying investment under CRA rules, the monthly loan payments throughout the year should be fully tax-deductible, right? Not exactly. Here's where things get a little tricky!

Return of capital means just what is says: your own money is returned to you in the form of a cash distribution. Since you used borrowed money to purchase the investment, the amount of interest paid throughout the year (e.g. $4,000) is eroded for tax deductibility and must be adjusted down in relation to the amount of distributions classified as ROC (i.e. $6,000). The calculation should account for the annual amount of ROC and will also have to be prorated throughout the year to reflect that the monthly schedule of ROC distributions.

TDMP-approved accountants track a running calculation of the effects of ROC distributions against interest deductibility and carry the balances forward each year to ensure that the schedules section of your T1 general tax returns will always be accurate.

Another adjustment required as a result of ROC distributions is on the adjusted cost base of the underlying asset. For tax purposes, you must reduce the cost base of the asset by the amount of ROC that was distributed throughout the year. In effect, this means that you will potentially create a future capital gains tax that will be deferred until you sell the mutual fund. In the TDMP, that is likely to be seven to ten years from the date you purchased it. In the meantime, you will receive the long-term growth benefits from having the money invested.

Deducting and deferring are the two most effective strategies you can use to reduce the amount of tax you owe. Borrowing to purchase assets that distribute ROC provides you with the opportunity to take advantage of both of these strategies. However, you should never gloss over the complexities of tax calculations; you should always engage professionals to ensure your tax filings are accurate and precise.

STAGE IV
The Home Stretch
(Be Your Own Banker)

It's the home stretch at last! You have reached the final stage in your journey to mortgage freedom. At this point, all your debt must be 100% tax-deductible because you have just completed the Tax Deductible Mortgage Plan (TDMP), and you will find that your financial priorities have once again changed and you must rebalance your portfolio. Specifically, you will no longer have any need for the TDMP Accelerator. This special-purpose investment vehicle has done its job and the monthly cash flow that was critical in converting bad mortgage debt into good debt is no longer required.

As the first wave of TDMP customers complete their debt conversion from bad-debt mortgage to good-debt investment line of credit, they start to think more about funding their retirement. As a typical example in the home stretch, we are going look at the options for a fifty-three-year-old couple who have a total net worth of $2 million. Their portfolio includes their home valued at $1 million, a $500,000 RRSP, a TDMP investment portfolio worth $1 million, and a $500,000 HELOC, which was used to finance the TDMP investment portfolio.

Since the couple in our example are still working, they have two new priorities in this final stage of their journey: 1) continue to apply the principles of responsible leverage to generate wealth in pursuit of personal financial targets, and 2) adjust the amount of leverage in the portfolio to the appropriate level for age and the time horizon to retirement. Clearly, these two goals seem to contradict each other and financial planning appears to have become a balancing act. Now that the TDMP is behind them, our couple wishes to keep the leveraged investments and set them to the new purpose of increasing their nest egg.

This section describes an option for becoming free of all debt without having to sell your investments.

Mortgage Freedom: The Ultimate Goal

Many homeowners, especially first-time homebuyers, will only think of a mortgage as the means to purchasing a home. At the beginning of your journey, your own cash reserves were only sufficient to make a down payment on a property, and the mortgage was the way to finance the rest of the purchase price and buy the home as described in Stage I of this book. Now that you're in the home stretch, you get to think of homeownership and mortgages in the reverse order. Rather than thinking of your mortgage as a means to acquire real estate, you must now realize that your mortgage also provided the means to invest in your nest egg.

Now, in your home stretch to retirement, the time has come to be free of all debt. Financial experts unilaterally agree that paying off your debt, including your mortgage, before you retire is a prudent thing to do. We start our journey to mortgage freedom very highly leveraged (e.g. 9:1 or 19:1) with a high-ratio insured mortgage when we are young. During our working years, we will transfer this leverage from our home to our retirement portfolio, which provides the added benefit of making the interest on debt tax-deductible. Then, in our final act before retirement, we expect to pay off all our debt and de-leverage our balance sheet right down to zero.

The mathematical geniuses at Yale University who wrote *Lifecycle Investing* have proven to us that you can retire with 63% greater wealth, with the same risk, if you borrow to invest when you're young rather than waiting to pay off your mortgage first. The principle of time diversifying our equity investments over thirty years using our home equity to borrow money in the early years is mathematically superior to the more conventional serial method of paying off the mortgage first and then starting to save. Canadian techniques including cash damming and the Tax Deductible Mortgage Plan (TDMP) are practical methods of achieving the promise of a wealthier, less risky retirement. You are at an advantage if you had the foresight and the good fortune to have implemented these mortgage and investment strategies and now find yourself in the home stretch to retirement with a significant head start. It's likely you have a much larger nest egg than your neighbours, who, in their fifties, may still be trying to pay off their mortgage and have not yet started to save much for retirement outside of their registered plans.

There are two clear options when it comes time to get rid of all your debt once and for all. You can choose to either sell some of your non-registered assets and pay off the debt entirely or you can keep all your investments and shuffle your own balance sheet around to place your mortgage (HELOC) debt into your RRSP with you (i.e. your RRSP) as the lender.

The first scenario of reducing your good debt by selling assets is a straightforward process. The key to this debt-reduction strategy is to sell assets while considering effective tax planning. Seek professional advice from your tax advisor and expect to execute your plan over multiple years to minimize your tax liability. Liquidating investments to pay off your debt may have adverse tax consequences if not planned properly. In our example, the fifty-three-year-old couple could liquidate a portion of their $1 million TDMP investment portfolio, sufficient to pay out the $500,000 HELOC, and pay the capital gains tax that results when assets are sold.

Their second option is much more interesting and a bit more complicated, as it involves using their RRSP and becoming their own banker. It should be noted that at the time of publication, this is strictly a "do-it-yourself" strategy, as there are no managed services yet available to assist you in becoming your own banker. However, there are currently at least three Canadian financial institutions that support this strategy and they are listed on the website at www .mortgagefreedom.ca.

Your RRSP: Be Your Own Banker

What if you could be your own banker? What if you could put yourself on the other side of your own deal and simply turn your debt into an asset? What if you could replace your lender with yourself by using your own RRSP? If you could achieve this, effectively becoming a lender to yourself, you can fully de-leverage your personal balance sheet without having to liquidate a portion of your portfolio to retire your debt.

Technically, there is no leverage in a scenario where you become your own banker because you're on both sides of the balance sheet and the risk is fully offset. You have some limited control over the interest rate that you charge yourself, and in the worst-case leverage scenario, where interest rates soar and markets underperform, you will be fully hedged.

Here's How It Works

For the purpose of this example, we will treat the RRSPs of our fifty-three-year-old couple as if they were a single registered plan. They own a home worth $1 million and have a $500,000 RRSP. Their TDMP portfolio is worth $1 million and is supported by a $500,000 tax-deductible HELOC that is secured by the home. The goal is to become debt-free forever without selling assets and to safely add another $500,000 to the retirement fund over the next ten years.

Currently, our couple has an asset allocation of 50% equities and 50% fixed income. The fixed-income assets are held in the RRSP, which is appropriate because interest can grow on a tax-deferred basis, and the equities are held in the non-registered TDMP investment portfolio, where distributions largely consist of dividends and capital gains, which are more tax efficient.

The first step in becoming debt-free and to avoiding having to sell assets that would trigger tax consequences is to liquidate the $500,000 worth of bonds and other fixed-income assets in the RRSP. The RRSP assets must be turned into cash in preparation to pay out the $500,000 HELOC.

The next step is to make an application for an RRSP mortgage in the amount of $500,000 (find out where at www.mortgagefreedom.ca), which must be approved by both the lender who will service the mortgage on behalf of the RRSP and the mortgage insurer who will protect the RRSP in the event of default. The RRSP grants our couple a fully open interest-only HELOC at 6%. The RRSP provides the $500,000 loan required to take out the existing HELOC. Voila! The couple is now debt-free—sort of.

The couple must now make a $2,500 interest-only monthly payment every month to the RRSP. As an investor, the RRSP has selected an interest rate that provides a satisfactory return for a fixed-income portfolio. Note that the rules for a non-arm's-length mortgage in a self-directed RRSP dictate that the interest rate must be "commercially reasonable." Matching the interest rate charged to the posted rate of large banks is prudent. The 6% interest rate used in our example is in reasonable proximity to five-year posted mortgage rates at the time of writing.

The couple may need to make the RRSP loan to themselves amortizing, but for the purposes of this example, let's assume interest-only payments to keep the math simple. Remember, 6% on a $500,000 loan equates to a $2,500 monthly interest payment (or $30,000 per year). The $30,000 collected by the RRSP constitutes a return on an investment already inside the RRSP and therefore *will not* affect their annual contribution maximum. The RRSP contribution room is still fully available for any new money that they have available to contribute to their plan. However, since the RRSP is charging more interest than the previous HELOC lender (e.g. posted rate), the couple may need to shuffle the assets in their $1 million non-registered TDMP investment portfolio to generate the cash flow required to cover the new mortgage interest payment (i.e. $2,500 per month).

The cash distributions from the TDMP investment portfolio will be mostly dividend income, which will be tax efficient, especially in retirement, where it becomes the only source of income, and will be completely offset by the federal and provincial dividend tax credits. In our example, the dividend income generated by the non-registered TDMP investments should be split between spouses with an eye to tax planning and with the advice of a qualified accountant. In retirement, these dividends will effectively be tax-free.

This is great news when you consider that the $30,000 interest paid to the RRSP is a tax deduction. The fact that the couple simply replace the old good-debt $500,000 HELOC with a loan from their own RRSP means that the

$30,000 of interest that they're paying into their RRSP annually is entirely tax-deductible in their own hands. At a 40% marginal tax rate, our couple will realize a first-year tax benefit of $12,000. Investing this money along with the $30,000 that they pay to their RRSP each year will allow our couple to comfortably reach their financial goal of safely adding another $500,000 to their retirement fund over ten years.

Risk

You should not be swinging for the fences with any of these investments. As long as you break even in your non-registered portfolio after collecting enough dividends to cover a $2,500 monthly mortgage interest payment, a non-arm's-length, self-directed, RRSP mortgage strategy is going to be worthwhile. If you follow our example in executing this strategy, you will have made your RRSP a winner (guaranteeing it a 6% return on a fixed-income investment) and your $12,000 annual tax refund is available to reinvest or spend at your discretion. However, you should be careful with the assumption that the RRSP return is "guaranteed." There is the potential risk that you, as the borrower, may default on your loan obligation to your lender, even though your lender is your own RRSP. Under what circumstance might you default on yourself? The answer, of course, should be never, but there is still a risk here.

The worst possible outcome of this RRSP mortgage strategy is the scenario where you lose your job or otherwise fall on hard times and are forced to default on the mortgage you're holding in your own RRSP. Can you imagine your own RRSP foreclosing on you? Your RRSP will take your home and throw you and your family out on the street. It will have no choice. As detailed below, government rules for these non-arm's-length mortgages force you to have a National Housing Act–approved lender administer your mortgage and collect the payments. If your mortgage payments dry up, your RRSP is going to treat you just as any other lender would: less than kindly! What's worse, because your RRSP isn't allowed to own property, after it forecloses, it will be compelled to sell the home that was formerly yours, probably at a discount to the market price.

If there's any silver lining in this perverse worst-case scenario, it would be that the federal government has actually provided an exception for Canadian registered plans to own property for a short period, but only in this exact circumstance (i.e. where it acquired it through foreclosure because of a mortgage default). While you aren't normally allowed to hold real property in your RRSP, in the unlikely event that your RRSP actually forecloses on your mortgage and ends up owning your home, the government will give your RRSP up to one year to unload it.

Another risk is that you may not find yourself as well diversified in your RRSP as you're used to, assuming your mortgage is taking up a lot of room. Also, your allocation of fixed income in your overall portfolio will have changed. You should consult your financial advisor on these issues before proceeding with this strategy.

Benefits and Costs

The risk of foreclosing on yourself aside, the benefits of

holding your own mortgage in your RRSP can be significant. The primary benefit of being your own banker is that you're able to keep your portfolio of leveraged investments intact while getting rid of all your debt. This is a beautiful way to de-leverage before retiring, as it means you don't have to face any potential adverse tax consequences of selling taxable non-registered assets to retire your HELOC debt.

While you may have had to liquidate some fixed-income assets in your RRSP to make room for your mortgage, your mortgage is going to outperform all of them as long as you set the interest rate high enough (within commercially reasonable parameters). You will need to budget for the costs to set this up and to operate it on an annual basis. Costs vary by financial institution and are available online at www.mortgagefreedom.ca. The costs are no different from the costs incurred by any lender in a normal mortgage transaction. The difference is that some of these costs are buried in the interest rate and you wouldn't be familiar with them. In general, you and your RRSP will need to budget a few thousand dollars for upfront costs that may include a lender application fee for the CMHC-approved lender, an appraisal, insurance, legal fees, and any other fees that may be required to move or setup a self-directed RRSP. There will be ongoing costs that the lender (i.e. your RRSP) will need to pay, which will erode the actual return that your RRSP nets after costs. Costs may be fixed at a few hundred dollars per year or they may vary at a small fraction of one percent of the size of the mortgage.

There is also an opportunity cost to the $500,000 in liquidated RRSP investments that would otherwise be performing at market levels, perhaps providing you a 2% to 3% return in times when that is about the best you can get from any GIC.

Another downside to this strategy is that it isn't easy to implement. Few financial institutions get excited when they receive an application for a self-directed RRSP, non-arm's-length mortgage, and you can't reasonably expect any financial institution to be highly motivated to help you achieve the goal of becoming your own banker. By turning your RRSP into a mortgage lender, you're competing with your bank! Most banks aren't interested in simply seeking the opportunity to collect interest payments from you every month for a small fee; they want to be your lender as well! After all, that's where the big money is. There are currently several Canadian financial institutions prepared to support this strategy. Information on service providers can be found at www.mortgagefreedom.ca.

When you place a non-arm's-length mortgage in your own RRSP, there are certain rules that you must follow, including:

- The trustee must be a CMHC-approved lender as defined by the National Housing Act.
- You must insure your mortgage through a national mortgage insurer (e.g. CMHC or Genworth).
- Mortgage terms and interest rates must be commercially reasonable (e.g. prevailing posted or discount mortgage rates).

When It Doesn't Make Sense

Being your own banker won't always make sense. A mortgage in your RRSP is neither liquid nor diversified. If an illiquid asset the size of the investment loan you're considering isn't a suitable investment for your RRSP for either or both of these reasons, then you shouldn't do it. The other issue is cost. Some of the costs in setting up an RRSP mortgage to yourself are fixed (i.e. they don't depend on the size of the mortgage) and it will run you several thousand dollars to set up the strategy in any event. Therefore, if your RRSP mortgage is too small (e.g. less than $200,000), it's probably not worthwhile to implement this strategy, as the fixed setup and operating costs will increasingly offset the benefits in proportion to smaller mortgage values. On the other hand, if you're planning to take out a substantial RRSP mortgage (e.g. $300,000 or more), the fixed costs begin to work in your favour and this solution becomes more attractive and increasingly cost effective with larger mortgage amounts.

To recap, if you just came through the TDMP and it's time to get rid of all your debt, but you're reluctant to sell your investments, then you should seriously consider becoming your own banker!

A Final Word on Advice

Good advice always has its place. Even if you're a do-it-yourself personality, you should remain open to accepting professional advice. Few would disagree that you should see a doctor when you're sick or you should see a dentist when you have a toothache. When it comes to your personal finances, why wouldn't you also seek advice from qualified professionals? The problem is that it's not always easy to separate good advisors from self-serving salespeople. A long history of this has driven many consumers to distrust anyone who charges for their advice.

Accountants and Lawyers

When seeking advice on an investment strategy, you probably shouldn't look to your accountant or lawyer for encouragement. You should certainly seek their advice in the context of their professional expertise, but you can't reasonably expect them to be supportive of an investment opportunity.

When you ask your accountant or lawyer for investment advice, what you may be doing (whether you realize it or not) is asking for a cheap insurance policy in case the investment doesn't work out. Any investment is going to come with some risk, and if it fails to deliver the result you were seeking, it would be nice to have someone to blame or even to sue to help recover your loss. Accountants and lawyers seldom give advice that causes them to take on undue liability—and why should they? You pay them the same hourly rate for their professional expertise either way, so the wisest thing they can do to limit their personal liability with respect to a solicitation to opine on an investment strategy would be to simply advise against the idea. A good accountant or lawyer with no specific knowledge in the field of investing would advise you to consult a specialist.

When you need tax advice, see your accountant. When you need legal advice or you wish to understand your legal liabilities, you should see your lawyer. For mortgage and investment advice, see below.

Mortgage Professionals

Mortgage advice should always come from a qualified mortgage professional. There is only one national standard in Canada, which is the Accredited Mortgage Professional (AMP) administered by the Canadian Association of Accredited Mortgage Professionals (CAAMP). AMP is the nationally recognized mortgage designation for all mortgage brokers, agents, originators, sub-brokers, planners, specialists, and the many other names by which mortgage professionals either choose to be called or are required to designate themselves under their respective provincial rules.

An AMP designation in itself does not guarantee anything but a good starting point and a base education. An independent mortgage broker/agent is much like an insurance broker in that they have access to a full range of mortgage products from many chartered banks and mortgage lenders. A reputable independent mortgage professional with the AMP designation will be the most helpful person to arrange a mortgage, suggest debt strategies, and assist you in navigating the mortgage application process. If in doubt, get a referral from a trusted friend or colleague. If that's unavailable, there is a list of high quality mortgage professionals and some further advice on this subject at www .mortgagefreedom.ca.

Investment Advisors

There are many different designations for financial advisors, and this can be a bit confusing for you as the consumer. A licensed financial advisor is regulated and insured and is required to have and maintain some level of proficiency in their specific area of expertise. For mutual funds, the Mutual Fund Dealers Association (MFDA) is self-regulatory body in Canada that boasts over 73,000 licensed mutual-fund salespeople in 138 dealers on their website at www.mfda.ca. An independent financial advisor must hold a licence as an "Approved Person" with a member of the MFDA before they are allowed to sell mutual funds.

Investment advisors employed by an IIROC-regulated (Investment Industry Regulatory Organization of Canada) dealership are licensed to offer a full range of financial securities, including stocks, bonds, and options.

Separate provincial regulators are responsible for licensing insurance brokers and mortgage professionals.

When seeking balanced advice, it's important to understand how an independent financial advisor is licensed and what they are able to sell. The old adage "when the only tool in your belt is a hammer, everything looks like a nail" can apply here. If your advisor is only licensed to sell insurance products, you shouldn't be surprised to find out that there's an insurance solution to every financial problem. If you ask an insurance advisor about investments, you'll very likely be offered a selection of segregated funds, which might look similar to mutual funds but are wrapped in an insurance policy and are therefore regulated as an insurance product and distributed through a licensed insurance broker. If your financial advisor is only licensed to sell mutual funds, then your investment options will be restricted to mutual funds. Many financial advisors are proficient and licensed to sell under multiple categories including mutual funds, insurance, as well as prospectus-exempt financial products. If you want to know the full range of products that are available through an individual financial advisor, you need to ask them what product categories they are licensed to represent and offer.

At the top of the food chain for investment advice is the portfolio manager. Sometimes referred to as an ICPM (Investment Counsel and Portfolio Manager), they hold the highest form of proficiency and experience and are regulated directly by their respective provincial securities commission. Portfolio managers perform the actual investment function on behalf of their clients, which means they actually buy and sell the financial instruments on their clients' behalf.

Financial Planners

A good financial planner will take a holistic view of your family balance sheet and cash flows and will ask you the right questions before presuming to provide any specific investment advice. Without the benefit of hindsight, there aren't going to be any obvious right or wrong answers with respect to specific investments. The only thing you can reasonably do is develop a set of criteria for making an informed decision each time. If you have a process in place for evaluating the pros and cons of any investment opportunity, you will make better choices. So how do you develop this process? The answer is you can't until you make a financial plan. You need to set strategic goals, make a plan, and then—and only then—will you have the framework to document the evaluation criteria that you will use to make tactical decisions on specific investments. Before you make any investment decisions or seek specific investment advice, you should make a financial plan.

There is no single national or provincial standard for financial planning in Canada, so it's important to seek credentials and references when engaging a financial planner for the first time. There are some 17,000 Certified Financial Planners (CFPs) in Canada. CFPs have a level of expertise and education that is administered by the Financial Standards Planning Council (FSPC). There are other financial planning industry organizations in Canada, such as the Financial Advisors Association of Canada (Advocis), which promotes its own designations, Chartered Life Underwriter (CLU) and Registered Health Underwriter (RHU), and recognizes the CFP designation.

You should seek financial planning advice from those who have the requisite experience and credentials. You will find further information on financial advisors and referrals to high-quality financial planners and mortgage planners at www.mortgagefreedom.ca.

Family and Friends

Trusted referrals from family members and good friends can be invaluable. However, investment or mortgage advice from unqualified individuals is worth less than zero.

Using your closest connections to get a referral to a qualified professional is one of the best ways to find a good advisor. This works well because when you make a referral, there is an underpinning expectation of performance. Nobody wants to make a referral to a friend or a sibling and have it turn into a disaster. That would be embarrassing. The real reason referrals from family and friends are generally reliable is that any advisor who has built a successful referral business is generally a more conscientious individual than advisors who get their business from business directories. They aren't necessarily better because they are smarter or more knowledgeable; they just tend to care more about their clients, or at least they care about their referral sources. Whatever the motivation, a professional who cares more because their business is heavily dependent on referrals is less likely to let you down than one who gains all their clients through brute-force marketing. This is by no means a truism, but, generally speaking, you're better off with a trusted referral than relying on a business directory to find your advisor.

When you retain the services of a lawyer, accountant, mortgage broker, or financial advisor through a referral, you become part of the professional's business network. If the consultation is less than satisfactory, bad news will burn through the referral network like a forest fire. Professionals who build their business on referrals can't afford this kind of negative word of mouth and will bend over backwards to prevent it.

In summary, don't ask friends and family for advice. As hopeless as you might be at advising yourself, you can reasonably assume that they are going to be just as bad. Just ask for a referral to a qualified individual that they trust and take it from there.

Parents

If you have a child in their twenties or thirties who is responsible enough and ready to buy their first home, consider giving them the down payment. The best financial assistance you can give your child is the down payment that gets them on the property ladder for the first time. If they buy a $200,000 home and you can give them $40,000, you will have set them on their way to owing a $2 million home and having a $2 million retirement fund, if they follow the strategies in this book, by the time they are your age!

If you can only afford 5%, or $10,000, to help them with their down payment, it's still better than letting them rent for the next ten or fifteen years. If the mortgage lender requires that you guarantee their payments, just make sure that you believe that they will actually make them and be prepared to help them with that too if they come up short of cash in the early years.

The sooner you can give your kids a leg up into homeownership, the sooner they will become financially independent. Also, make sure they read this book!

Conclusion

The road to mortgage freedom is a strategic journey throughout most of your working life. Paying off your mortgage faster is an intuitive impulse, but it may not be the most direct path to building the substantial nest egg that we all need to retire in comfort.

The authors of the book *Lifecycle Investing* prove to us mathematically that if you borrow to invest for retirement at a young age, you will increase the value of your retirement portfolio by 63% as compared to waiting to save for your retirement when you're debt-free. *Mortgage Freedom* adopts the principle that being invested in equities over a longer period will improve your prospects at the end of your working life. It provides a practical method for Canadian homeowners to set their mortgages to a better purpose and achieve all their financial goals. This book challenges you to try and think of financing your retirement the way you financed your home.

Success breeds confidence and, as Canadians, we seem

to be supremely confident investors in real estate, especially when it comes to our own homes. When we purchase our first home, it's common to use 9:1 or 19:1 leverage, and we fully anticipate that this routine application of high-ratio mortgage debt in our early years will reward us handsomely with a home we intend to own mortgage-free by the time we retire. The concepts presented in this book suggest that your confidence in borrowing to buy your home should be transferable to your retirement fund along with your mortgage. A side benefit of aligning your mortgage with your long-term investments is that debt will become tax-deductible and generate considerable additional wealth through tax benefits.

The endgame of the mortgage freedom strategy will see you owing your own home, free and clear of all debt, as well as amassing a considerable fortune that will allow you to retire comfortably. Using a mortgage to finance a nest egg may be the only way to achieve this goal for many Canadians.

This book describes the journey to mortgage freedom in four stages. In Stage I, you will get on the property ladder by purchasing your first home. You aren't making a long-term plan at this stage. Ask an independent mortgage professional to advise you on how much house you can afford to buy (including the mortgage), then find an appropriate home and buy it.

Once you have de-leveraged into the conventional zone (i.e. less than 4:1 loan-to-value ratio), it's time to start Stage II and the debt conversion process called cash damming. Move your mortgage over to your retirement fund in small monthly increments and start the investment process as early as you can.

In Stage III, you hit the gas by rapidly accelerating the process of converting your mortgage into a tax-deductible investment loan using the Tax Deductible Mortgage Plan (TDMP). The TDMP was first introduced to the Canadian market in 2006 by the author.

In Stage IV, you will enter the home stretch to retirement. You can pay off your tax-deductible HELOC by selling some investments, or you can simply liquidate some T-bills or other fixed-income assets in your RRSP and shift your own mortgage over to replace them. Paying mortgage interest to yourself is a much better solution than paying the interest to your banker. Take back your mortgage from your lender and become your own banker. This will allow you to fully de-leverage before retirement while keeping your entire investment portfolio intact.

If you find yourself in your forties or fifties by the time you read this book, fret not. You can apply the strategies set out in Stages III and IV directly. If you have already paid off your mortgage, you can still use the strategy in Stage IV of using your RRSP as a source of cash to build a non-registered investment portfolio to redouble your efforts and retire with the funds you need.

If you think more strategically about your mortgage debt, you will realize there is a material opportunity to put it to work to bulk up your nest egg for retirement at every stage of your working life. Forget the serial five-year mortgage program that your bank loves to sell you. Forget paying off your mortgage while ignoring your retirement fund. Think strategically and prepare a holistic financial plan with your financial advisor. Visit the website at www.mortgagefreedom.ca for a referral to an advisor or to join the conversation about *Mortgage Freedom*.

Mortgage Freedom is your journey to financial success. Make your own good fortune.

Epilogue

As a computer engineer, I've always been passionate about technology. The inspiration for *Mortgage Freedom* has its roots in this passion combined with a constant curiosity in how we can apply technology to fundamentally transform and improve our lives. My curiosity has led to several ventures over the years, but none so interesting and compelling and as the Tax Deductible Mortgage Plan (TDMP), which I co-founded in 2006 with my wife, Kim, and my brother, George.

Every few years, technology provides us with a whole new set of game-changing tools, and from time to time, we get to witness a few brave (and often reckless) visionary souls attempting to use these tools to build something useful. These individuals stand to be rewarded if their product makes a difference in people's lives, but for the most part, their efforts will go unnoticed and unrewarded.

After two decades of software development, the TDMP was the venture for which we were eventually rewarded. The

TDMP has helped thousands of ordinary Canadian home-owners recover over $5 million dollars in wasted tax dollars and has shown them exactly how to collect and use this money to bootstrap their underfunded retirement plans. The TDMP is our reward. My father says that I was born lucky!

Let me tell you a story. Once upon a time, I was an eager young army officer with a brand new degree in computer engineering. I was charged with the responsibility of purchasing the Canadian army's very first "microcomputers." I remember it so clearly because I had just been promoted to the rank of captain and was delighted to get the opportunity to put my education to good use. Delighted is an understatement. Getting the opportunity to acquire and configure a new generation of "personal computers" was the most exciting thing that could ever have happened to a computer geek like me in those days. But what stands out the most in my memory of these days was the staggering cost of hard drives for these revolutionary new computers.

This was a brand new generation of technology that ran on Intel's 386SX microprocessor, and the disk storage units for these computers were removable and had to be purchased separately. The cost of each single 10MB hard drive was $10,000! Granted, these hard drives were designed to a military specification that added to the cost, but the fact remains that the cost of computer storage back then was $1,000 per megabyte! In October 2010, I purchased a 500GB replacement hard drive for my laptop computer for $500. That's $1 per gigabyte or one tenth of a cent per megabyte of storage.

Think about it! The cost of 10MB of computer storage

has plummeted from a lofty $10,000 twenty years ago to one single penny today. This phenomenon is directly attributable to Moore's Law. In 1975, Intel co-founder Gordon Moore famously forecasted that the number of transistors that can be placed inexpensively on an integrated circuit would double approximately every two years. Amazingly, this has turned out to be more or less true, and the trend is widely expected to continue in the years to come.

We have seen the impact of this exponential enabler of computing technology across all industries, and there is no greater example than the cost of computer storage dropping by a factor of one million, from $10,000 for 10MB twenty years ago to a single penny today. It's astonishing to consider that a single gigabyte (i.e. 100 x 10MB hard drives) of computer storage would have cost $1 million back in the day.

The impact of this exponential growth of technology has been nothing short of staggering and has completely reformed the computer and telecommunications industries. The cost of long-distance telephone lines and computer storage used to be the major expenses that shaped the computer industry. Twenty years ago, the simple task of downloading and storing a high-definition movie from a server on the other side of the world would have taken months to accomplish and cost millions of dollars in long-distance phone bills and hard drive storage. Today, thanks to the Internet and as predicted by Moore's Law, it's not only possible to download a movie from a server on the other side of the world, it streams in real time and is practically free!

Moore's Law is about to do for the financial services industry what it already did for the Internet and telecommunications industries. The impact that computer technology will have in the financial services sector over the next two decades will be nothing short of profound. What does the future hold for the ordinary Canadian homeowner as technology continues to drive down the variable cost of financial transactions and improve the online experience?

The Internet has already opened our eyes, empowering Canadian homeowners with real-time mortgage and investment information and online access to a plethora of other financial products and services. We have witnessed explosive growth in online trading as the quality of service and access to information improves. Transaction costs continue to plummet each year. How low do you think transaction costs can go? Perhaps zero!

More than 100,000 people in this country go to work every day with the single purpose of providing advice on mutual funds and mortgages. This isn't surprising when you consider that more than 5.6 million homes are mortgaged to the tune of $1 trillion and Canadians hold over $600 billion in mutual funds. Over the next decade, technology is going to drastically change the way all these people work. Things are already starting to change. The free-falling variable cost of computerized financial transactions, driven by Moore's Law and the explosion of Internet services, is putting power in the hands of consumers. Product knowledge is power and it used belong to financial professionals, but it has been transferred to anyone who can simply google it! Where's your value in the workplace in this new future? I believe we are going to see two distinct job functions emerge to service the upcoming generation of sophisticated Internet-enabled homeowners and investors.

The first is a rapid growth of comprehensive financial planning: complete lifecycle advice that takes a holistic approach to financial planning and considers both sides of the personal balance sheet. Consumers are starting to demand that their advisors be more helpful. The appetite for complex financial strategies that help save taxes and build wealth is going to grow and sophisticated consumers are going to seek advisors who can help them achieve their long-term goals, not just get them a mortgage or sell them some mutual funds.

The future of independent distribution for Canadian financial products will be increasingly in the context of holistic comprehensive financial planning. My advice to future financial advisors is to check all the financial planning boxes: get your CFP, your AMP, and your insurance proficiency. If you want to specialize, be sure to join a financial planning firm that offers it all! The combination of a CFP designation with an AMP designation is powerful and will empower the financial professional of tomorrow with the tools they will need to keep up with the demands of increasingly sophisticated homeowners.

Good investment advice for ordinary Canadian homeowners who still have a mortgage remains hard to come by. Historically, the best investment advice comes from fully experienced and well-qualified portfolio managers. As a practical matter, this has only been available to high-net-worth individuals and institutional clients. By definition, if you still have a mortgage, you will not meet the minimum threshold of wealth required for direct access to first-class investment advice. This is also about to change.

In the past, the best advice was reserved for institutions and individuals with $5 million dollars or more to invest. Advances in technology and software have systematically driven this threshold down, first to $1 million dollars, then half a million, and recently we've seen the bar dip as low as the $100,000 range. As Moore's Law marches on and the technology improvements follow, it's inevitable that the ordinary Canadian with only a small sum to invest should someday have equal access to the advice currently reserved only for the elite investor with millions of dollars. Technology drives efficiency in all markets, and as the spread between bond yields and the cost borrowing continues to collapse, new products and services will increasingly become available to the ordinary consumer on favourable terms.

While growing up, I always knew that I wanted to be an engineer. At seventeen years old, I joined the army and attended the Royal Military College of Canada (RMC), which had the finest academic program for computer engineering students in the country. An education at taxpayer expense comes with the opportunity to serve one's country, and I'm proud of the eleven years I served as a young soldier at the pleasure of Her Majesty. Perhaps that is why my personal charity of choice is Canada Company.

Founded by Honorary Colonel Blake Goldring, chairman and CEO of AGF Management Limited and AGF Trust, Canada Company provides a wide range of support to our men and women in uniform. The Canada Company

Scholarship Fund was set up to finance a university education for the children of military personnel who lose their lives in active service. By purchasing this book, you have contributed to this worthy cause, as a portion of the royalties will be donated to Canada Company. Thank you for your generous contribution, and best of luck on your personal journey to mortgage freedom!

Yours truly,

Sandy Aitken

Afterword

When I began my career as a mortgage professional in 1999, the world was a much simpler place. Back then, when a client needed a mortgage, they would phone or fax me and I would arrange it with a lender. Today's homeowners are more confident and sophisticated, and they demand much more than the simple mortgage advice of days gone by. Over the last ten years, I have personally arranged thousands upon thousands of mortgages for my clients, funding over one billion dollars of debt secured by their residential property. I have watched the demands of my customers change over the years.

Increasingly, my clients began to seek my advice on how to structure their mortgages to finance their investments, whether in business, property, or markets. Fortunately, new mortgage products started to appear in response to this demand, especially multi-component home equity lines of credit (HELOCs) and collateral-charge mortgages, which allowed for both fixed and variable mortgages to be combined under one mortgage. My business has flourished in response to my clients' demand for better advice, not only about their mortgage but also about taxation, investing, and cash flow management.

What makes our team different is that we truly strive to integrate someone's mortgage into their short- and long-term financial goals. In the pursuit of that vision, we have reviewed and examined every known personal finance strategy regarded as beneficial to consumers available in the marketplace today. In fact, it's all we do each and every day.

Enter Sandy Aitken and fast-forward to 2011. I have known Sandy personally for over ten years, and it has been inspirational to watch him build his business in the mortgage industry. Sandy is a pioneer who had a vision to develop a turnkey mortgage, investment, and tax solution on a technology platform at a time when the mortgage, investment, and tax professionals were entirely independent and rarely worked together. Sandy realized, as I did, that consumers seeking mortgage advice from independent professionals would increasingly expect a more holistic approach to financial planning based on their overall cash flow, payment, and net worth objectives.

The Tax Deductible Mortgage Plan (TDMP) is unequivocally the most comprehensive and hassle-free way for consumers to realize and benefit from these strategies, as well as many of the other tactics enclosed in this book. TDMP.com is regarded as the industry standard for flawless execution of the TDMP by both homeowners and industry professionals alike. The company has won numerous mortgage industry awards and appeared on *Profit Magazine*'s coveted Profit 100 list of Canada's fastest growing companies in both 2009 and 2010.

In writing *Mortgage Freedom*, Sandy Aitken has done quite literally to the mortgage process what the lifecycle theory of investing did to consumer awareness of investing—established with certainty that there is a higher probability of accumulating greater wealth with lower risk by integrating an investment strategy with a tax-efficient mortgage plan. Many personal finance books will tell you *what* you should do, but few will actually explain *how* you can actually do it. *Mortgage Freedom* is a practical guide for Canadian homeowners on *how* to proactively manage debt and build greater wealth for retirement.

The results are undeniable, the facts are irrefutable, and the tools are now in your hands. My advice to you is simple: visit TDMP.com and take the TDMP Test today! Integrating your mortgage, wealth management, and tax strategy will require some effort, but the benefits may very well make a difference for quite literally generations to come.

Calum Ross is ranked as the top producing mortgage broker in the country by Canadian Mortgage Professional (CMP) *magazine. He is regularly featured in the media as a mortgage expert, including appearances on Canada AM, City TV, BNN, and Inside Toronto Real Estate. He is the mortgage columnist for* New Homes and Condos *magazine and is regularly quoted in newspapers such as the* National Post, The Globe and Mail, *and* The Toronto Star. *He holds both a B.Comm and MBA in finance and is currently completing the Comprehensive Leadership program at Harvard Business School.*

Appendix: Key Court Cases

The Duke of Westminster

Rule 1. Taxpayers may order their affairs to minimize the amount of tax payable. [Commissioners of Inland Revenue v. Duke of Westminster (1936) A.C. 1 (H.L.)]

In this English case, the Duke of Westminster executed deeds of covenant in favour of certain employees, promising to pay them weekly sums for seven years in recognition of past services. At the time the deeds were signed, the employees were receiving fixed wages. After the signing, employees who continued to work for the Duke got such amounts as, when added to the sums payable by the deeds, totalled the amount of the wages payable before the deeds and no more. The Duke paid surtax, a higher rate of tax payable by wealthier individuals. Wages paid to employees are not surtax-deductible, whereas payments made under deeds of covenant are. The Duke claimed the deduction. The Revenue proposed that there was a doctrine that the Court may ignore the legal position and look at the substance of the matter, i.e., that this was just another way of paying wages, fabricated to allow the Duke to claim the deduction. The Court rejected the Revenue's proposition and said that the substance is what results from the legal rights and obligations of the parties, ascertained upon ordinary legal principles. An individual (the Duke in this case) is entitled to arrange his affairs to reduce his tax liability. This decision by the House of Lords, England's highest civil court of the period, enshrined this principle and precedent for future cases.

This case was brought up in the Lipson case (see below).

Shell Canada

Rule 2. The complexity of arrangements by taxpayers do not affect Rule 1. [Shell Canada Ltd. v. Canada (1999) 3 S.C.R. 622]

This case involved sophisticated corporate finance transactions, which we need not go into detail here. The gist of it is that Shell claimed tax deductions for interest paid under s. 20 (1) (c) (i) of the Income Tax Act, and the CRA (formerly Revenue Canada) denied the claim, saying the Court should consider the "economic realities" of the case. It's a similar argument to that used by the Inland Revenue v. the Duke of Westminster (see above).

This is, in part, what was ruled:

However, this Court has made it clear in more recent decisions that, absent a specific provision to the contrary, it is not the courts' role to prevent taxpayers from relying on the sophisticated structure of their transactions. [...] Unless the Act provides otherwise, a taxpayer is entitled to be taxed based on what it actually did, not based on what it could have done, and certainly not based on what a less sophisticated taxpayer might have done.

The Singleton Shuffle

Rule 3. A taxpayer cannot be denied a benefit simply because their transaction was motivated for tax-planning purposes. [Singleton v. Canada (2001) 2 S.C.R. 1046, (2001) S.C.C. 61]

This is the leading case on interest-deductibility planning. John Singleton, a partner in a Vancouver law firm, withdrew capital from the partnership (his equity therein) and used the money to assist in the purchase of a house. He then borrowed the same amount from a bank and used it to repay the partnership. For tax, he deducted the interest on the money borrowed from the bank on the basis that he used the money to earn income from the partnership. The Court accepted that the interest was deductible because the direct use of the borrowed money was to contribute capital to the partnership, even though Singleton conducted the transactions to buy a principal residence.

This type of arrangement—sometimes called the "Singleton Shuffle"—is acceptable tax planning. There are further comments about it in the Lipson case (see below), where the general anti-avoidance rule (GAAR) was discussed at length. However, GAAR didn't figure in the Singleton decision because Singleton's transactions occurred before GAAR became law.

The Lipsons Lose but Taxpayers Win

Rule 4. It could be argued that the rule in the Lipson case is that there are no rules. [Lipson v. Canada (2009) S.C.C. 1, (2009) S.C.R. 3]

Mr. Lipson wanted to buy a house using borrowed money. At the same time, he wanted to make the interest paid on the money tax-deductible against his income. If he took money from the family corporation he owned, he would be taxed on the distribution. If he used mortgage proceeds to buy the house, the mortgage interest wouldn't be tax-deductible. He proceeded by a series of transactions with his wife as follows.

She borrowed $562,500 from the bank, which she used to purchase shares in the family corporation from her husband. He transferred the shares to her and he then used the money she paid him for the shares to purchase a house in their joint name. That same day, the Lipsons obtained a mortgage of $562,500 on the house and Mrs. Lipson used this money to pay off her bank loan. At this stage of the proceedings, the Lipsons had successfully made their mortgage interest tax-deductible, notwithstanding the fact that these transactions were designed to obtain this tax benefit. The Lipsons avoided tax, and at this stage, they were entitled to do so.

Justice LeBel, speaking for the majority, in his reasons for the judgement, stated that it had long been a principle of tax law that taxpayers may order their affairs to minimize the amount of tax payable. He cited the English case decided in the House of Lords, Commissioners of Inland

Revenue v. the Duke of Westminster (see above). This long-standing principle has been given in answer to those who may think that there is something wrong with seeking ways to proceed within the law to reduce one's tax liability. Further, in relation to the deductibility of interest at this stage of the Lipsons' process, LeBel had this to say:

> [...] we must consider the tax benefits conferred on Mrs. Lipson by ss. 20(1)(c) and 20(3), namely the entitlement to deduct the interest. In my opinion, the respondent has not established that in view of their purpose, these provisions have been misused and abused. Mr. Lipson sold his shares to his wife and bought the residence with the proceeds of that sale. [...] In the result, Mrs. Lipson financed the purchase of income-producing property with debt, whereas Mr. Lipson financed the purchase of the residence with equity. To this point, the transactions were unimpeachable.

So at this stage in the Lipsons' transactions, all is well. In fact, the tax planning so far is similar to that in the Singleton case. However, far from confirming that Rule 3 as it applied in the Singleton case could be applied to all planning situations, Lipson distinguished Singleton, as Singleton was not a GAAR case. Also, the Lipsons relied on the spousal attribution rules (i.e. it was Singleton with a "spousal twist").

LeBel avoided the question of whether the Singleton strategy is acceptable, but seemed to approve the Singleton situation as it occurs in Lipson up to the point where the Lipsons sought to rely on the spousal attribution rules.

We are entitled to take from LeBel's dicta that Singleton is okay but Lipson went further. Then the Lipson case went on to hold that, notwithstanding Rule 1, we must consider GAAR, and using the relevant sections of GAAR, the majority concluded that the Lipsons' use of the spousal attribution rules was "abusive" and the tax deductions claimed by them were disallowed. The dissenters argued that the majority's interpretation of GAAR in this case would lead to uncertainty for tax planners, to which the majority replied that uncertainty is inherent in cases of this kind (i.e. cases involving the analysis of GAAR rules as they apply to the particular facts).

The outcome of all this, as far as can be seen, is that:

1. Singleton-style planning—arranging one's affairs to use capital to purchase a residence and borrowed funds to invest—is still acceptable;
2. nothing changes the rules for the individual taxpayer adopting a strategy within the Income Tax Act to obtain a tax deduction; and
3. financing the purchase of personal assets from equity and investments out of borrowings is allowable.

Nina Sherle: It's Not What You Do, It's the Way You Do It

Rule 5. In executing a tax plan to obtain tax deductibility on payments made, a taxpayer must be careful to take purely legalistic steps—even though contrived—to ensure interest deductibility under the Income Tax Act. [Nina Sherle v. HM The Queen, an appeal at the Tax Court of Canada before the Honourable Justice J.E. Hershfield.]

Nina Sherle had two houses: 1) the Joyce property, which was both her residence and unencumbered, and 2) the Ewart property, which was both rented out and mortgaged. She wanted to switch houses, and live in the Ewart property and have it unencumbered, and rent out the Joyce property.

She borrowed on the security of her former residence (the Joyce property) to enable a switch of properties, i.e., to pay off a loan on the Ewart property, formerly a rental property, so that she could move into it as her new residence (mortgage-free) and rent out the Joyce property. She sought to deduct the tax on the mortgage interest, relying on subparagraph 20 (1) (c) (i) of the Income Tax Act, which sets out the requirement that, for interest on borrowed funds to be deductible, the borrowed funds must be used for the purpose of gaining or producing income.

The CRA argued successfully that the actual use of the borrowed funds was to pay off a mortgage on the new personal residence and the interest was therefore not deductible. The judge, somewhat reluctantly, had to agree—reluctantly because Sherle could have arranged her affairs another way to achieve the same result and qualify the interest as tax-deductible, but she didn't. She could have sold the Joyce property and moved into the Ewart property, using the cash from the sale to pay off the mortgage on the Ewart property. She then could have taken out a mortgage to buy another rental property, or perhaps even buy back the

Ewart property if that were possible, although that might be unwise in view of GAAR (see below).

This case shows that care must be taken in these tax plans to follow the letter of the law, notwithstanding that the overall result might be the same.

General Anti-Avoidance Rules (GAAR)

The extensive discussion of GAAR in the Lipson case won't be examined here, as it doesn't strictly relate to the Singleton situation (i.e. structuring finances to obtain an interest deduction when purchasing personal assets provided that the purpose of the borrowed money is to earn income from a business or property). This was approved in the Lipson case. The only reason for raising GAAR here is that it has caused confusion in the minds of many—tax planners and mortgage brokers among them—who seem to think that Lipson and its pronouncements on GAAR are a deterrent to adopting a Singleton-style tax plan.

The purpose of GAAR is to deny a taxpayer tax benefits achieved by a plan that complies with the letter of the law but amounts to abuse of its provisions. It's not meant to apply to all tax planning. Three conditions must be satisfied for GAAR to apply:

1. There must be a tax benefit resulting from one of the transactions implemented.
2. The transaction must be an avoidance transaction (i.e. the only purpose of the transaction is to obtain the tax benefit—the transaction has no other non-tax purpose).
3. The transaction, or series of transactions, must be abu-

sive (i.e. inconsistent with the object, spirit, or related provisions of the Income Tax Act).

Clearly, if one of the purposes of a transaction is to invest and build up a fund for retirement, the transaction isn't an avoidance transaction under the above condition 2.

The CRA had argued that GAAR reversed the result in the Singleton case, denying the interest deduction. In the Lipson case, the Supreme Court concluded that there was no misuse of the interest deductibility provisions of the Income Tax Act.

Tax planners must be mindful of the application of GAAR, but effective tax planning is now more important than ever in the preparation of a long-term financial plan.

Notes

1. *Annual State of the Mortgage Market in Canada* published by Canadian Association of Accredited Mortgage Professionals (CAAMP) in November 2010.

2. IT533 Interest Deductibility and Related Issues, Canada Revenue Agency www.cra-arc.gc.ca, 30 October, 2003.